Notting Hill Editions is an independent British publisher. The company was founded by Tom Kremer (1930–2017), champion of innovation and the man responsible for popularising the Rubik's Cube.

After a successful business career in toy invention Tom decided, at the age of eighty, to fulfil his passion for literature. In a fast-moving digital world Tom's aim was to revive the art of the essay, and to create exceptionally beautiful books that would be lingered over and cherished.

Hailed as 'the shape of things to come', the family-run press brings to print the most surprising thinkers of past and present. In an era of information-overload, these collectible pocket-size books distil ideas that linger in the mind.

Ian Nairn (1930–1983) was a British architectural critic and topographer who made his name with a special issue of the *Architectural Review* in which he coined the term 'subtopia' to describe the areas around cities that had, in his view, been failed by urban planning, losing their individuality and spirit of place. In the 1960s he contributed to the volumes on Surrey and Sussex in Nikolaus Pevsner's *Buildings of England* series and wrote a number of his own books, including *Nairn's Paris* and *Nairn's Towns*, both published by Notting Hill Editions. He also presented several BBC television series. His work has influenced writers as diverse as J. G. Ballard, Will Self, Iain Sinclair and Patrick Wright.

Described by the *Guardian* as 'one of the country's finest pop-culture historians', Travis Elborough is the author of many books, including *Wish You Were Here: England on Sea*, *The Long-Player Goodbye*, *Through the Looking Glasses: The Spectacular Life of Spectacles* and *Atlas of Vanishing Places*, winner of the Stanford Illustrated Book of the Year in 2020.

OUTRAGE

Ian Nairn

–

Introduced by
Travis Elborough

nh Notting Hill Editions

Published in 2024
by Notting Hill Editions Ltd
Mirefoot, Burneside, Kendal LA8 9AB

Series design by FLOK Design, Berlin, Germany
Cover design by Tom Etherington
Creative advisor: Dennis PAPHITIS

Typeset by CB Editions, London
Printed and bound by Imak Ofset, Istanbul, Turkey

First published by The Architectural Press, 1955

A CIP record for this book is available from the British Library

ISBN 978-1-912559-63-3

nottinghilleditions.com

This book is a reprint of the June 1955 Special Number of the *Architectural Review*. The issue started by being called *Outrage in the Name of Public Authority*, but in collecting the material it became clear that the issue was much wider, and that we are all offenders as well as victims. Public authorities are responsible for nearly all of the faults exposed in this issue; they have most power and often least awareness of the visual responsibility that should go with it, but they are only a corporate reflection of what goes on in the mind of each one of us. So the title of the issue became simply *Outrage*; and the Outrage is that the whole land surface is being covered by the creeping mildew that already circumscribes all of our towns. This death by slow decay we have called Subtopia, a compound word formed from suburb and utopia, i.e., making an ideal of suburbia.

Contents

In this reprint of the *Architectural Review* is uttered a prophecy of doom – the doom of an England reduced to universal Subtopia, a mean and middle state, neither town nor country, an even spread of abandoned aerodromes and fake rusticity, wire fences, traffic roundabouts, gratuitous notice-boards, car-parks and Things in Fields. It is a morbid condition which spreads both ways from suburbia, out into the country, and back into the devitalised hearts of towns, so that the most sublime backgrounds, urban or rural, English or foreign, are now to be seen only over a foreground of casual and unconsidered equipment, litter and lettered admonitions – Subtopia is the world of universal low-density mess.

The *Review* attacks this situation on visual grounds, which are its proper province, but philosophical justifications for a categorical condemnation of Subtopia are not wanting. Man's triumphs of conscience and consciousness have been achieved at the cost of a specialisation that has cut him off from the rest of nature. His mental and physical health require that he shall be able to recreate himself in environments that are conspicuously nature-made, not man-made,

that he shall be able to distinguish wild from tame, country from town. Subtopia smudges over this vital difference,
destroys country without making town. Britain is a small
and over-loaded island where the natural scene is already at
a premium, but patches of spreading Subtopian blight are
already beginning to coalesce, minor thoughtlessnesses are
beginning to agglomerate into a major disaster. To battle with
this amorphous destroyer is a daunting task, but bigger problems are being tackled in other fields, and something must be
done, now, because the alternative is the abyss.

– Agents –

13

Subtopia is made with human artefacts, often inoffensive in
themselves, disastrous in the places, quantities and associa-
tions in which they are found. Within the town the agents
of Subtopia are demolition and decay, buildings replaced by
bijou gardens, car-parks and underscale structures, reduction
of density where it should be increased, reduction of vitality
by false genteelism, of which Municipal Rustic is the prime
agent, the transporter of Subtopian blight to town and country alike, as is the badly detailed arterial road and its accompaniment of crank-necked concrete lamp-posts. The essential
ancillaries of the road, garages and cafés, falsely genteelised
and casually sited, merely spread Subtopia instead of func-
tioning as elements in a coherent transport pattern. Public
bodies lend their support to the spread, draping wire across
town and country indifferently, for power, light or fencing
– this last a speciality of the great super-agents of Subtopia,
the Ministries of the Crown, with their camps and dumps,

aerodromes and atom-plants; whether in use, but widely dispersed, or disused, but not cleaned up; bringing Subtopia to areas that might have seemed remote from attack.

– Route Book –

49

A black guide to England along a line ruled across the map from Carlisle to Southampton. A line that passes through no great conurbations or other areas where blight might confidently be expected, but nevertheless finds in town and village and once-unspoiled country Subtopian indifference and thoughtlessness visibly expressed in malpractices that can be photographed and located on the map, documentary proof that Subtopia is all around us, and a warning that we can afford to take no isolated objects for granted because we are already approaching a density of such objects when they can no longer be taken as isolated, at which point it is already too late.

– The Highlands –

129

Britain's last great reservoir of non-Subtopia, of rugged unspoiled landscape that is as natural as one can have it, lies in the Highlands of Scotland, an area that must gain increasing importance as the psychological balance to the Subtopian south. Certain things need to be done for the inhabitants of the Highlands – they need power and light and social services – but an opening-up of the Highlands to industry and charabanc tourism would be their ruin as a reservoir of wilderness. Action is needed now, for spots of Subtopian infection have already appeared, in the form of insensitive forestry, badly designed and ill-sited hydro-electric plant, thoughtless road building and plain suburbanism in house design.

– Summing Up –

What must we do to be saved? These pages offer a Manifesto and a call to action, a programme, precepts and a check-list of malpractices for which the opponents of Subtopia must be ever on the alert. The programme calls for the development and the enhancement of the differences between places, it is oriented toward topographical responsibilities, rather than administrative ones, what can be seen rather than what it says on a piece of paper. Decisions, private or departmental, affect the ground around us every day, may place a site in jeopardy, may require immediate action. That action must be directed to the right quarter, and in the right tone of voice, but it is needed now, and from all of us. The defence of the individuality of places is the defence of the individuality of ourselves.

– Anthology –

TRAVIS ELBOROUGH

– Introduction –

The book you hold in your hands was the making (if quite possibly ultimately the breaking) of the brilliant architectural writer and broadcaster Ian Nairn. It first appeared in June 1955, initially as a standalone, if incendiary, edition of the *Architectural Review* magazine entitled *Outrage*, but was rapidly reissued as a book. (As you will discover 'the *Review*' itself is sometimes spoken about in the third person throughout the book.) Nairn was just twenty-four and so a full year ahead of John Osborne's jazz-loving Jimmy Porter he was hailed in the national press as the prototypical angry young man. What irked this Brillo-haired young upstart, however, was not the Church, the Sunday papers and a posh wife insistent on the ironing, but the sorry state of Britain's built environment. It was a topic that consumed him for the remainder of what proved to be a furiously productive (or perhaps more accurately, productively furious) if tragically all-too-short career. Succumbing to alcoholism, driven by melancholic despair, he was to drink himself to death twenty-eight years later. By which time he was a largely forgotten figure, despite briefly being as familiar a face on television as Sir John Betjeman.

With Nairn it is sometimes too easy to become fixated on that end and the unfulfilled potential. The grim stories of liquid lunches at the St George's Tavern pub near his home in Pimlico, where pints were consumed by the dozen almost daily. All those books promised (*Nairn's London Countryside*, *The Industrial North*, *Nairn's Florence*) that never materialised and the tide of beer that gradually swept away his much-cherished pilot's licence, a regular berth at the *Sunday Times* and any further work at the BBC and finally, after lapsing into a prolonged silence, his life, in 1983 at age fifty-two. But this is to overlook how much he achieved and the impact his extraordinary writing had on the general public of his day – and far beyond.

Proclaimed as a 'prophecy of doom', *Outrage* exploded like a grenade in the shabby genteel world of mid-fifties Britain. A nation where rationing had only recently ended and a decidedly-past-it Winston Churchill just retired as prime minister, but compulsory national service for men aged between seventeen and twenty-one was to rumble on for a further eight years. And a jolly good thing too, the disgusted of Tunbridge Wells most probably felt: what with flick-knife-wielding teenage Teddy Boys menacing every Essoldo Cinema and Locarno Ballroom in the land and no tea-chest or washboard safe from the attentions of skiffling would-be Lonnie Donegans, if Fleet Street was to be believed.

If the country still bore the scars of a conflict that

had ended nearly a full decade earlier, with its towns and cities bomb-cratered and those demob suits not yet discarded entirely, a growing sense of impatience with the make-do muddling through the status quo is clearly discernible at this juncture. *Outrage* is in so many respects an expression of that impatience. And not least with the sort of dead hand the officious military, with their fondness for wire fencing and keep-out signs (WARNING – DOGS PATROL AT NIGHT, etc.), evidently continued to exert over swathes of England's green and not-so-pleasant land. While Nairn was to note 'the appalling rash of huddled huts on the sky-line' at the enlarged American airbase at Greenham in Berkshire, more invidious to him was the loss of common land which he rightly deemed 'the new form of an old battle – Enclosure'. The common, thirty years later the locus of the women's anti-nuclear protest encampment, was not to be returned to open public use until 1997.

But then the ill-effects of the services on the landscape were something Nairn was more than familiar with. Late in life (and even afterwards, since it was cited on his death certificate) he claimed Newcastle as his birthplace. Yet he had been born in Bedford in 1930, as his father was an engineering draughtsman employed at the Royal Airship Works in nearby Cardington. When the works closed after the R101 went up in flames on its maiden voyage that October, the family moved to Frimley, a quarter of leafy west Surrey pockmarked by defence establishments, and which Nairn subsequently credited with instilling in him a 'deep hated of characterless buildings and places'.

Nairn would go on to survey most of his home county for the Surrey volume of Nikolaus Pevsner's *Buildings of England* series. Though unlike Pevsner, or his contemporary and *Architectural Review* colleague Reyner Banham, he had no formal education in architecture, having studied mathematics at the University of Birmingham before signing on with the RAF as a pilot officer. It was while he was stationed in Norfolk and flying Gloster Meteor jets that Nairn began writing pieces on architecture for the *Eastern Daily Press*. His ideas about buildings and their environment were always informed by this formative experience of observing them from the air.

On-spec articles, followed up by a concerted letter-writing campaign, along with (once he'd left the RAF and moved to London) doorstepping the *Architectural Review*'s offices in Queen Anne's Gate, Westminster (which for Nairn had the added appeal of its own pub, The Bride of Denmark, in the basement), finally resulted in a job as the assistant production editor on the magazine in July 1954.

By then what would eventually become the *Outrage* issue was well underway. Encouraged by its mercurial proprietor-editor Hubert de Cronin Hastings and John Betjeman, a former *Architectural Review* assistant editor himself, both of whom had been leading the charge against the cluttering of Britain by unsightly signage, concrete lamp posts and chain-link fencing, Nairn had already spent some three or four months working on a piece bearing that title. (Hastings would write a chunk of the introduction to *Outrage* and most likely also compiled the 'Anthology' of time-worn quotes at the end, thereby bookending the issue editorially, as perhaps was only his right.)

A visit to a new housing estate in Headington in Oxfordshire earlier that spring had first spurred Nairn to coin the term 'subtopia' for a morass of new developments that he believed were slowly erasing any difference between the town and country. What was emerging, to his mind, was a sort of homogenising suburbanisation on steroids that resulted, as he would write, in 'the steamrollering of all individuality of place to one uniform and mediocre pattern'. Seeking to test his thesis, and with Hastings' blessing to expand on the theme, he undertook a journey north from Southampton to Carlisle (with a further sojourn to the Scottish Highlands, almost as a palate cleanser since Nairn hailed it 'the last great reservoir of non-subtopia'), armed with a pile of spiral-bound notebooks and the office Leica camera to record what he encountered.

The routes of those journeys were to provide the backbone to, and meat of, *Outrage*. Its overarching rallying cry was similarly shaped by them. And that cry presciently shrieked, that without action, it would not be long before 'the end of Southampton' looked like 'the beginning of Carlisle' and 'the parts in between' like 'the end of Carlisle or the beginning of Southampton'.

As perhaps is the way in all such ventures, there was a certain degree of what we'd now call confirmation bias in this odyssey. Nairn went looking for the underwhelming, the dreary, the mediocre and all-out bad and offensive and was not to be disappointed. But then there was much to be disappointed by. *Outrage* is upfront about this, describing itself as 'a black guide to England' and works like a kind of a Baedeker in reverse. Page after page is a catalogue of eyesores rather than beauty spots, backed up with photographic evidence (shot by Nairn himself) and bold graphics and illustrations, all arrestingly laid out by the *Architectural Review*'s innovative arts editor Gordon Cullen. (Sadly the particular size and black-and-white format of this edition means a few elements of Cullen's design have had to be compromised, but we've tried as far as possible to stay true to his original scheme, and equally to preserve the grainy beauty of Nairn's photography, albeit within the limits of our scale.)

The overall effect, in any case, is somewhat like a cavalcade of holiday snaps from somewhere closer to hell than any picturesque paradise. The reader was able, if they felt so inclined, to follow in Nairn's dismal footsteps (or tyre-tracks, actually) with the section-by-section route maps across the country provided.

There is a field guide element in the mix too, with I-Spy-style photo spreads intended to serve as 'a checklist of malpractices', on the likes of 'wire' ('wire obliterates the pattern of the countryside just as surely as though it were a blanket of semi-detached housing'), 'dumping grounds', 'arterial roads' ('. . . can be beautiful. These aren't'), 'airfields', 'things in fields', 'advertising stations' ('the attempt to art them up is ten times worse than anything Horrid Commerce can do') and what he termed 'rural municipal rustic'. The latter was the kind of cod-countrified beautifying of bypasses and their ilk by local authorities on the rates that Nairn damned as 'Look, we are spending your money wisely, we have dug a little plot, isn't it nice?'

As this final sarcastic put-down suggests, local authorities, too often guilty of favouring expediency over excellence, along with other government agents, with their misguided father-knows-best, anti-urban ideas about good taste, were among the chief kicking boys of *Outrage*. But Nairn's most radical proposition, and foreshadowing more contemporary appreciations of edgeland landscapes, was to suggest that in certain instances instead of attempting to camouflage chaos at a town's fringe, it might be better to intensify it: 'More industry, housing and wire not less to give a ring separating town and countryside.'

Outrage was to conclude with a four-page manifesto, intended as a call to arms 'for the man in the street, rather than for architects and planners'. One that nevertheless attracted some rather higher profile supporters almost immediately. Within days of the issue hitting the newsstands, the Duke of Edinburgh, Prince Philip, had referred to 'subtopia' in a speech. The Duke was then seen as quite the trendsetter, socially and sartorially, with the *Daily Mirror* around this time promoting him as a style icon for sporting handmade 'suede-shoes with thick rubber sponge soles' – Teddy Boy 'creepers' by any other name. But in a far more deferential age, his words carried real weight and Nairn and subtopia were suddenly front-page news.

Invitations to appear on television to be grilled by the notoriously testy Gilbert Harding, then celebrated by a waxwork effigy in Madame Tussauds that labelled him 'The Most Famous Man in Britain', duly followed and a six-part series entitled 'Journey Through Subtopia' was to air on the BBC's World Service. In May 1955, the Architectural Society of the University of Liverpool staged its own exhibition of local photographs entitled 'Outrage' in the war-damaged church of St Luke's, its opening attended by Nairn who accused the city's architects of 'trying to level everything to grey haze' and 'of being afraid to do something noble and positive and intelligent' and therefore 'blundering into a style of compromise and platitude'. More famously, two years later students at the Royal College of Art, inspired by a lecture Nairn gave at the school, formed the Anti-Ugly Action group and staged a run of flamboyant protests against buildings they disliked, such as Kensington's new Neo-Georgian public library by E. Vincent Harris. More lastingly *Outrage* gave rise to the establishment of the Civic Trust, initially chaired by the Conservative politician Lord Duncan-Sandys, which as late as 1961, the *Guardian* newspaper, if rather sceptical of its results, still maintained was 'Waging the war against subtopia'. Typically Nairn, who to the end prided himself on his independence, refused to join. Perhaps to the detriment of his health but to the enormous benefit of his work as a critic, he was to remain utterly unclubbable, forever siding with the *hoi polloi* against the architectural profession and the supposedly great and good. Just over a decade after *Outrage*'s publication, and having grown ever more disillusioned, Nairn was to issue a 6,600 word screed in the *Observer* entitled 'Stop the Architects Now!'

Outrage is inevitably a work of its time, a period when the need to rebuild remained urgent and the paternalistic desire to make the world anew had a unique potency. Nairn issued his opening salvo some seventy years ago and he could never have foreseen the near-complete disappearance of industry and manufacturing or the arrival of out-of-town retail parks, city-centre student accommodation silos (the generic-Tesco-metro-metropolitan, if you will) and distribution hubs. Let alone a digital-enabled present that often privileges the virtual and the distant over the near and real. Commercial television had yet to begin broadcasting in Britain when *Outrage* was published, after all. Nairn was writing before limits to the heights of buildings in London had been abolished and when politicians of all stripes, including the newly re-elected Conservative administration under Anthony Eden, were fully committed to the continued mass building of council homes and the creation of a second wave of new towns. At the time of writing, new towns are seemingly back on the agenda, lending Nairn's observations about them in *Outrage* a renewed topicality. Yet in terms of what we've ended up with so far, our world surely looks never more subtopian. And if Nairn were alive today, arguably mendacious commercial property developers and their enablers rather than municipal authorities and government bureaucrats would most likely be in his sights. Some of the targets of *Outrage* have naturally gone, its route maps chart mostly vanished territory, an A-road Britain without a single motorway to call its own, but its polemical power is undiminished by age. Dismay alas continues to be a valid response to much of what surrounds us.

This is the first and last view of rural England to be seen in these pages. It is just a reminder of what we are squandering with all the means at our disposal, confident that there will always be some left over. What follows proves this is a criminally feckless illusion, and that we are in fact obliterating the whole countryside.

– Subtopia –

T his issue is less of a warning than a prophecy of doom: the prophecy that if what is called development is allowed to multiply at the present rate, then by the end of the century Great Britain will consist of isolated oases of preserved monuments in a desert of wire, concrete roads, cosy plots and bungalows. There will be no real distinction between town and country. Both will consist of a limbo of shacks, bogus rusticities, wire and aerodromes, set in some fir-poled fields: Graham Greene's England, expanded since he wrote in the 'thirties from the arterial roads over the whole land surface. Upon this new Britain the review bestows a name in the hope that it will stick – SUBTOPIA.* Its symptom will be (which one can prophesy without even leaving London) that the end of Southampton will look like the beginning of Carlisle; the parts in between will look like the end of Carlisle or the beginning of Southampton.

How has this come upon us? Britain is an industrial country. Britain has a population of 50,000,000 crammed into an island which could take 25,000,000 decently. Britain is top-heavy. Industrialisation has created an 80 per cent urban majority. Popular misunderstandings of one sort and another – misunderstanding of the meaning of democracy – vulgarisation of the concept of liberty – have led the man-in-the-street to kick against the principle of land planning.

False tolerance, likewise, has led him to tolerate every kind of abuse in the name of free competition or public expediency. There's a lot of unspoilt country, the feeling runs, and sooner or later the population graph will level out and even take a dive and then urban spread will cease. A fallacy. Spread is dependent no longer on population increase but on the services a power-equipped society can think up for itself. With radio and supersonic speeds you get the capacity for infinite spread, the limiting factors of time and place having ceased to operate. The city is to-day not so much a growing as a spreading thing, fanning out over the land surface in the shape of suburban sprawl. However, something even more sinister is at work: applied science is rendering meaningless the old distinction between urban and rural life; the villager is becoming as much a commuter as the citizen; the old centres of gravity have been deprived of their pull at both ends and in the middle; no longer geographically tied, industries which once muscled in on the urban set-up are getting out of the mess they did so much to make, and making a new mess outside. The arterial road has developed a way of life of its own with its own ribbon-type development – villa, 'caff', garage, motel, caravan camp – carried into the heart of a countryside which is under sentence to machine agriculture.

This thing of terror, which will get you up sweating at night when you begin to realise its true proportions, we have called, as we say, Subtopia. It consists in the universal suburbanisation not merely of the country, or of the town, but of town-and-country – the whole land surface. Suburbia becomes Utopia, Utopia becomes suburbia.

This is not to say suburbia has no place in the scheme of things. The review has from time to time regaled its readers, to the dismay indeed of some, with the charms of the suburban ethos. What is not to be borne is that that ethos should drift like a gaseous pink marshmallow over the whole social scene, over the mind of man, over the land surface, over the philosophy, ideals and objectives of the human race; for this is what it is doing. And it is doing it not only as a psychological but a physical, a geophysical phenomenon. Not in England merely, in Europe, Asia, Africa, the Americas. Before the eyes of Frank Lloyd Wright in his hide-out in the Arizona Desert now runs a complicated pylon network. In the Pampas, once synonymous with the vast liberty of nature, areas the size of Britain are cut up by rectangular wire fences not unlike those that have completed the downfall of the once open downs of our own country. The same fate is overtaking the Highlands of Scotland. Australia boasts a wire fence a thousand miles long. Holland is already a suburb, Switzerland a hydro. Baghdad has trams. The Alps feed Italy with power that comes in endless chains of pylons over every mountain pass; the Dolomites are a vast hydro-electric scheme. Even in darkest Africa the warpaint and the tom-toms are no longer much more than an act put on for film companies and V.I.P.s.

Look where one may, in the East or the West, every background, no matter how sublime, has now to be seen against a universal foreground imposed by modern man, of posters, wire, disused petrol pumps, car parks, conifers, institutions for the insane, cement works, sanitation plants, generator stations, the wreckage of wars and War Departments. Right down to what the *Review* in this issue calls Things in Fields. All this adds up to a way of life for the people who live with these objects which is neither agricultural nor urban, but Subtopian.

Well, why not? Is there something wrong with the Subtopian way of life? The *Review*'s function in life is not philosophical but visual; its job is not to attack Municipal Rustic via the spiritual frustrations of a Black Country mayor, nor the grid wires by exposing the unrewarding life of an Electricity Board Commissioner. For the purpose of this issue outrages are classified in terms rather of the eye than of psychological disorder. Still, to meet the accusation that this method of approach is attacking from the surface inwards – which it is – it might be wise to say a word on the deeper issue.

Let us remember then that Nature is not to be

denied. There is a nemesis prepared for those who ignore this simple fact. The roots of humanity lie in something more basic than a kosikot; the absurdities of good-earth cultists should not blind even rational men to the limitations of reason. It isn't merely that human nature can't live for ever on bricks and mortar. Nor is it merely that – whatever the charms of herd life and mass psychology – latent within every human breast is the craving to escape, if only for a season, from the eternal friction with other minds. It is more than that. The fate of the human race is to be of the universe but isolated from it – out on a limb of the tree of life by reason of its specialisation of self-consciousness. The need to re-integrate the self-conscious identity with the unconscious universe, the need to return down the limb to the immortal trunk, to re-identify the human with the non-human, including the animal, world, in the shape of what Stapledon calls 'the simplicity, the severity, the silence and the beauty of nature', is the prime condition of personal re-creation.

Of this distinction between the self-conscious world of men and the un-self-conscious universe of nature, *town* and *country* are the equivalents in colloquial speech; the one man-made down to the last marmalade top, the other, man-modified or not, still carrying a bias weighted in favour of the unconscious part of 'creation'.

If this is so, the corollary, clear enough already to the sociologist and planner, should not remain hidden from the man-in-the-street. His duty to his background (far more than a duty in a crowded island, an elementary precaution) is twofold: on the one hand, to bring to the highest pitch of effective life his man-made environment – the 'city' – on the other, to put such limits to it as enable him to keep contact with the wild – the 'country'.

You can, of course, say this can't be done when the pressure of population grows as great as ours, but that is to ignore the landscape moral of the eighteenth century where every city did that very thing with a pocket handkerchief of a park.

What the eighteenth century did individually the twentieth can and must do collectively. Here lies the real challenge to modern planning, and there isn't much question what that challenge is. Everywhere where the borough engineer cracks the town wide open with road-widening and the local council obliterates the market place with a useless flower-garden, and everywhere outside where one department or another dumps a camp, a housing estate, or a sewage disposal plant into the indifferent wild – everywhere we are levelling down two ideal extremes (both necessary to our felicity) to a uniform mean: a mean which is a threat not simply to our felicity but to our continued development as more than an order of termites.

Why we are creating this mean of two extremes is equally clear. The environment is an extension of the ego, and twentieth-century man is likewise busy metamorphosing himself into a mean – a meany – neither human nor divine. And the thing he is doing to himself and to his background is the measure of his own mediocrity. Insensible to the meaning of civilisation on the one side and, on the other, ignorant of the well-spring of his own being, he is removing the sharp edge from his own life, exchanging individual feeling for mass experience in a voluntary enslavement far more restrictive and permanent than the feudal system. This heritage to which he is heir, a great heritage, product of centuries not in fee to mass psychology, the meany is busy breaking down. The pages that follow are the record of his success to date, masquerading as Improvement, Progress or Amenity. To say it again, it is man enslaved dragging down his environment to his own level.

And planning machinery is being used to speed Subtopia, not check it. The planning offensive was started in a mood of idealism which assumed two things: that rules would be used flexibly and intelligently, and that England was of unlimited size. This last, single, radical miscalculation gave rise to the whole philosophy of dispersal – expanded towns, New Towns and every house with a garden, which is now the mainstay of official planning policy: an admirable idea *in vacuo*, and implemented in perfect good faith, but condemned before it started by our coast-to-coast dimensions. Now the tail is wagging the dog, the Brave New World has been twisted to become the decanting of overspills evenly throughout the country – Subtopia.

Any hope of intelligent interpretation was lost when planning was tied down step by step with local government, and made into another unrewarding office job. This chained it to the very points where democracy is most likely to give the lowest common denominator, not the highest common multiple: corporate Subtopia with all the planning rules as its armoury, perverted to make every square mile indistinguishable.

In 1950 the *Review* traced this rake's progress, both planned and unplanned, in some of its manifestations in the U.S., a piece of research which drew from some of its American readers subdued applause but raised the blood pressure alarmingly in others. Unnecessarily, since the fact that we are all in this thing together, first as the victims and then, in varying degrees, as the offenders, is the first thing we have to know about it.

Here the *Review* (as it promised then) turns the searchlight upon this country. We have tried to play fair. To pick and choose special areas of blight like Corby would be too easy and would lay the argument open to the accusation of special pleading. To avoid that accusation we have put a ruler across the map of England and Scotland and drawn a line as straight as main roads permit from the bottom to the top – from Southampton in the south through Carlisle on the Border to the Highlands. The line from Southampton to

Carlisle we have followed in strides of 25 miles to a page in an effort to present a typical cross-section of the country – of the *countryside*, one might say, for the aim has been to choose a line which avoids the great conurbations. A line which, in fact, avoids the worst.

It shows, roughly speaking, two stages in the progress of the disease. First, main-road England, the limbo of shacks, bogus beautification, wire and radar stations, set in unhappy pastoral scenery. In the second part the Highlands themselves show the blight less advanced, much more thinly spread – and all the more noticeable since the outrages are isolated sores upon an awe-inspiring background rather than a rash of pimples amongst mildly complaining water meadows. With this is linked the thesis that here at least modern man has not yet trampled on the previous balance between man and nature; there is thus still time to make the Highlands a pointer to a saner visual world and a lung for the island's fifty million – a very different thing from the mixture of piecemeal industry, hydros, motels and charas, that some would like to impose on the Highlands.

Nevertheless, how widespread, how universal, is the feckless couldn't-care-less attitude of our whole society is seen as clearly in the far north as the far south; no remote Scottish loch but is ringed with a scum of sawn-off tins and shredded gumboots, lying where they were thrown to rot by the proud Gael. As we have said, we are all in this thing together. Look north, look south, you see either the services or the excreta of Subtopia.

The moral is not the Simple Life. A return to more primitive conditions is wanted by few of us; the ultimate objective of all industrial civilisation right down to canned beans and mod. con. is not to make Simple Lifers of us but to simplify our lives.

But because all the sustained scientific planning that goes into every industrial process or commercial undertaking stops short at the land surface, the colossal advantages that should be available are dispersed. The more complicated our industrial system, and the greater our population, the *bigger* and *greener* should be our countryside, the more compact and neater should be our towns. For if our urban sprawl and unplanned technology has squared since 1900, our potential, in ingenuity and techniques, for dealing with it has cubed. Too complex a problem? Not a bit of it – aircraft engineers are solving worse problems every day, and often producing visually wholesome results as a by-product. Surely we can manage to produce a little order by exerting all our powers? The alternative, quite clearly presaged in the sixty pages following, is the abyss.

Subtopia on the March: the morning after the battle, with pockets of field pattern awaiting mopping up. The whole country is beginning to look like this, as all development follows the same pattern of a careless romp of dispersal across the countryside, a pattern which is wasteful and dreary in itself and utterly impracticable in a small and crowded country.

11

The effect of several agents of Subtopia acting in concert, as shown in Gordon Cullen's drawing below, is only too familiar. Yet singly the eye may try to take them for granted – a fault which this section is attempting to counteract by abstracting them and showing them next to their counterparts in the next county.

– Agents –

S ubtopia is the annihilation of the site, the steam-rollering of all individuality of place to one uniform and mediocre pattern. In travelling up our route, the first impression would be of a chain of assaults on particular sites, each with its own problem, and this is presented on pp. 49–125. But Subtopia has already gone so far that it is possible to present scenes which have become indistinguishable, and to classify the causes which have made them look alike. These causes are the agents of Subtopia.

Most of them are unwitting agents, what Lionel Brett has called the diagrams of progress, put into the environment purely as means of transmitting electricity, or improving communications, and treated by their authors as though they were invisible. With these in themselves the review has no quarrel at all. Each diagram of progress is a challenge to be taken up; intrinsically neither bad nor good, but capable of producing visually bad or good solutions. The equation that produces Subtopia out of a good idea is always the same: the *mass application* of *misunderstood principles*. That is one reason – if a negative one – for adopting the functional tradition for a vernacular of trim; it is least likely to be misunderstood, because it is common sense. To deny progress is as lunatic as the situation to which uncontrolled progress has brought us: we are *enfants de notre siècle*, and if we regard the march of progress with a mannerist compound of admiration and disgust, well, we are *enfants de notre siècle* in that too. Hereafter, if pylons and arterial roads and lamp standards are objected to it is because they represent bad solutions, not because they are bad in themselves; *except* – and this 'except' will recur throughout the issue – where, because of overcrowding, the whole land surface looks like being submerged by them. This 'density clause' is why the review objects to the power station at Hams Hall on page 80, and its corollary, that the wild places must be kept really wild, is the reason for the quarrel with the quarry and A.A. Hut at Honister on page 120.

Most of the agents are unwitting, but there are two classes that aren't. One could fairly be called the Bye-law and Borough Engineers' Subtopia: the attacks on towns in the name of slum clearance, which spread sprawling estates in the suburbs, and leave the centre a collection of vacant lots. The other is the panic reflex to the spread of Subtopia, which attempts improvements using standards which are themselves Subtopian. Municipal Rustic, and the unhappy extension of Municipal Rustic back into the country along the roads. These two things are both wrong in their manifestations and wrong in themselves: typically they are the things least often regarded as eyesores. It is the great industrial plant that incites horror, however good its design, and not the cosy, but no less certain, break-open of the town with gardens and prettified car parks.

Finally, the agents are shown acting together in Standard Fringes. In the other groups there is sometimes enough character of landscape or townscape in the backgrounds for one to be able to guess where they are. That felicity has disappeared in this last set, and the review invites you on page 45 to a bitter guessing game. Is this the best that all the architects, builders, engineers and planners of England can do? The *Review* believes that it isn't; and its suggestions appear at the end of the issue. But buildings affect people, and Subtopia produces Subtopians – the *Review* also believes that, unless we are shocked into awareness, the consequences of our visual laissez-faire may make us incapable of distinguishing good from bad, and we may be mutated into sub-humans without our ever knowing it has happened. It's not just aesthetics and art-work: our whole existence as individuals is at stake, just as much as it ever has been from political dictatorship, Left or Right; and in this case the attack is not clearly defined and coming from the other side of the globe, but a miasma rising from the heart of our collective self.

Lamp standards

This is the agent that has most hope of being improved; and it has in fact been improved in the last year (see AR, December, 1954). However, any improvement will not affect this sorry stalk of poles for some time, and the first point about Subtopia is brought out straightaway: it is often largely a matter of trim. Functional trim like this is a means not an end: the end is – or should be – the main street of Kirkham, 12, or open country near Blackrod, 11. So it should be neat, clean and unobtrusive.

This is just what all these aren't: the reason – the usual one in matters concerned with England's appearance – is a combination of out-of-hand standardisation and expediency. Standardisation – 25-foot poles on main roads, 15-foot on minor roads – produces the fittings of incredible size well above the roofline (1, 4, 14, 15). Expediency provides the concrete – steel shortage – and the clumsy designs. Quite a plausible ancestry: almost respectable – until you look at the results and see Warwick's Georgian main street beaten up with right angles, 4, and the dormers of Abingdon town hall competing with a 25-foot pole with a broken neck, 2. They stamp any scene in which they appear with their own apathetic pattern, and if the scene is fragile, as Warwick is, or having a hard time to stay intact anyway, like Blackrod, it disintegrates.

There is in any case a built-in handicap in making neat slight poles out of concrete – it just *won't*, it's inherent in the performance figures – why not try tubular steel instead?

Key: 1, Southampton. 2, Abingdon. 3, Oxford. 4, Warwick. 5, Leamington. 6, Castle Bromwich. 7, Trent Vale. 8, Stoke-on-Trent. 9, Nantwich. 10, Warrington. 11, Blackrod. 12, Kirkham. 13, Kendal. 14, Kendal. 15, Cockermouth. 16. Carlisle.

1, 2, 3, 4

5, 6, 7, 8

9, 10, 11, 12

13, 14, 15, 16

Arterial roads

Arterial roads are necessary, and they can be beautiful. These aren't; they have become the projection of mediocrity from one town to the next – a means of prolonging the Standard Fringe to be a Standard Ribbon. The roads have extended the suburban boulevard that was the way they left the town, instead of looking at the site and arriving at the blend of tautness and local conditions, a very different thing. The essentials, as far as they can be stated away from a specific site, are Green Edges, Clean Edges and No Nibbling: whether the roads are thoughtless cut-rate widening, fully fledged motorways or Beautified roads like those shown on page 44.

Green Edges means an end to the concrete footpath in 10, a brutality not justified by 'the density of regular pedestrian traffic from Carlisle to Penrith', and also to the loophole in legislation which makes possible the provision of service roads a few feet from the main road without the result being called ribbon development, 6. The absurdly wide centre strip in 9 eats away the border space without preventing dazzle or being green enough to act as a foil itself. Either no borders and compactness, or wide green borders and a foil, but not diminuendi of the road fading away to the hedgerow: parts of A34 have six metalled streaks dumped across the view, 2 and 7. *Clean Edges* means the exercise of simple good manners by tidying up and not leaving the roadside as a dusty exposition of local geology, 1, and *No Nibbling* means the repression of signs like those in 1 and 6, carted wholesale from the Subtopian fringes into the middle of the country. Some signs are needed: others – like 5 – say just twice as much as is necessary.

Key: 1, A339, near Newbury. 2, A34, Bladon, Oxon. 3, A34, Yarnton, Oxon. 4, A34, near Chipping Norton. 5, A452, Coleshill. 6, A452, Castle Bromwich. 7, A34, Gailey, Staffs, 8, A580, St. Helens. 9, A6, Preston. 10, A6, High Hesket, Cumberland.

1, 2, 3

4, 5, 6, 7

8, 9, 10

The philosophy of the bad arterial road is split-and-dump, and the drawing below shows both aspects: splitting the hillside, cutting church from churchyard and maiming the roadside trees. In return it brings poles, wire, shacks and signs from the fringe of one town and scatters them all the way to the next.

Most military installations are a necessary evil, but the drawing here shows how aircraft can also spread Subtopia in an extra dimension and through an extra sense. Even away from the airfield, the sight and sound of the six-engined bomber and the formation of fighters can devalue a stretch of countryside, when repeated long enough and low enough.

Dumping ground 1

The way in which island sites collect a scrapheap of signs, as demonstrated by four Midland examples (1–4). The result is rather like coming across part of a junk yard carted into the middle of the road. Lack of co-ordination runs through them, each authority with its own pole, so that the Public Conveniences in 1 has a bigger pole than the signpost, and an inadequate sign in 4 has necessitated a makeshift 'Warrington' in wood. Duplication and redundancy run through them – the two beacons in 2 when there are kerbside beacons and zebras already; the multiplication of Keep Left's in 3 – three visible at one time, doubled with arrows, when one arrow was all that was needed. Small things but in a crucial position, and simple use of a pair of eyes and a pair of removal men could clear up so much of it.

Key: 1, Leamington. 2, Kenilworth. 3, Rugeley. 4, Knutsford.

Dumping ground 2

Using the whole road length as a dumping ground producing an endless chain of cafés and garages like these. They are a natural function of the road and should be encouraged, but not as a continuous ribbon through open country. Gathered together in knots at junctions and tidied up (though a squalid transport café is far less offence than a genteel one), they become elements in a coherent transport pattern as the staging posts used to be.

The Density Clause operates as usual; the number of motorways must be restricted or the whole country will become like the strip of Herts., south of St. Albans – pastoral countryside carved in all directions by routes out, routes in, by-passes and links. There is also an Indemnity Clause – these roads must guarantee that the old network in between remains unexploded. The danger is not in the motorways themselves, but in the application of arterial principles by local authorities to every country road regardless of site: Subtopia.

Key: 1, Burghclere, Hants. 2, Hampton-in-Arden, Warwicks. 3, Bassett's Pole, Staffs. 4, Lymm, Cheshire.

Airfields

Any type of military installation could have been chosen. They all reproduce the same pattern – new extensions and old derelictions; but only airfields impinge on the countryside through the sky as well as the land. Just how they impinge is shown on the map overleaf, ten miles either side of that part of the route which snakes up through the Midlands. The black blobs represent airfields, old and new; the blue circles indicate the circuit areas of those airfields that are in use – the areas in which one could expect to see and hear aircraft consistently under 1,000 feet. Those areas are beginning to coalesce. Again these airfields are necessary and inevitable diagrams of progress – though in only four of the seventeen can it be said to be peaceful progress. This doesn't automatically make them any better – the only crisp engineering job of the whole lot is Upper Heyford; the only neatly camouflaged airfield, and that incredibly well done, like a Repton park, is R.N. Culham – and that looks like the remote, still potent influence of the Nautical Tradition.

What, however, of the others? The twenty-three airfields marked on this map that did a useful job in the war, and are now too small, too near other airfields or redundant. There are so many that they could never all be used at the same time for fear of collision. Of these, as far as is known, three have been cleared up ten years after the war – the small grass training fields. Of the others, about six are dumps and one is an atom factory (Harwell), one trains parachutists and nine are derelict: turned back to agriculture but with the black pattern of runways, dispersal pens and hangars unmodified, the hutments not cleared away, one more element in the standard Subtopian countryside. This, remember, is only one part of one of the Services, to say nothing of the Ministry of Supply. As is said again later in the issue, and it can bear endless repetition, it is no use being prepared against attack if in doing so you destroy what you are supposed to be defending. Obviously we must have airfields but obviously also, they ought to be well designed, tidily detailed and landscaped into the countryside, and it is only common decency to tidy up as you go along, and not pack England tighter and tighter with abandoned runways and derelict huts from the latest war, accompanied, as often as not, by 'Air Ministry Property, No Trespassing!'

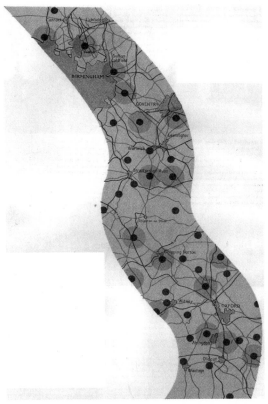

The black circles indicate airfields. The light grey circles indicate conventionally the circuit areas of the airfields. They are of standard radius based on a mean of light aircraft and A-bomber, and bear no relation to the actual size of the circuit used by the aircraft normally based at each airfield.

Wire

Wire obliterates the pattern of the countryside just as surely as though it were a blanket of semidetached housing. The view becomes wire and pylon first and site second, 12. In some cases it becomes wire and pylon everywhere and site nowhere, 1, 2, and 13: Subtopia.

Wire in a town blurs the form of the buildings and the shape of the street, whether it belongs to the GPO, 8, the bus company, 10, the electricity company, 6, or the neighbour's telly, 3. It reduces all urban scenes to the same common denominator − the lowest: Subtopia.

Though one can become accustomed to a little wire, one grid line, 12, or even one wire can spoil a whole view. In any case there is a density above which the self-erected defences cave in, and the mind becomes aware that the whole scene is covered with wires and poles: Subtopia.

The proper use of wire is in a fence, as a light precise demarcation. If the fence is made long and high to keep people out or military stores in, it covers enough of a view to superimpose its grid on the whole scene, 1 and 11 (which the park wall never did − it robbed you of one space but gave another, the volume bounded by it and the road). The latest U.S. version has started marching across country in 3-D, 5: Subtopia.

How much more of an indictment does one need?

Key: 1, Bicester Garrison. 2, Stockbridge. 3, Worthy Down, Hants. 4, Abingdon. 5, Brize Norton. 6, Woodstock. 7, Brownhills. 8, Penkridge. 9, Mexford, Staffs. 10, Leigh, Lancs. 11, Culcheth, Lancs. 12, Beetham, Westmoreland. 13, Carlisle.

Wire and trees

How modern man can reduce both technology and nature to the same type of meaningless ugliness.

Key: 1, Witney. 2, Grove, Berks. 3, Chandler's Ford, Hants. 4, Highmoor, Oxon.

Trees

A sad cruel little story, maiming trees in the interests of uniformity, making living things grow to rule for the sake of the rule. There are necessary causes for lopping, which may not always be obvious from a look at the site (though nearly all ills can be cured by pruning, maintaining the shape and reducing the density, not hacking off regardless at x feet y inches), and some trees are born to be pollarded. For that reason this is not a selection up and down the route, but a saw-cut through one town just off it – Witney – where the trees really do seem to be reduced to a standard height regardless of type, site and appearance.

There isn't much to say that isn't self-evident from the photographs. What should be self-evident to Witney is the implication – that if the out-of-hand application of a rule gives results like this, then the rule is wrong, not the trees; and the implication of that implication, that the attitude of mind which exalts rules over the reasons for making them is wrong too. It will erode lives just as it has eroded the town's appearance – they are internal and external manifestations of the same thing: Subtopia.

1, 2,
3, 4

Anti-urbanism

the town: 1850

the town: 1950

Urban sprawl has come to its second stage; with everyone gone to the suburbs the centre has been left to decay. Towns have become half-alive: one half is where you work, but can't live, the other half is where you live but don't work. Half-alive towns will produce half-alive people, and the most immediate result is that in between working and living there can be up to two hours of limbo, nearly fifteen per cent of one's waking hours: forced and frustrating comradeship in public transport or forced and frustrating isolation in private cars.

That sounds like lunacy, and it is only a statement of the social muddle, not the visual one. It would be no better if the estates on the fringes were beautifully designed and models of urbanity or augmenting the site; it is so much worse that they aren't, and that the original social reason for the whole futile business has fallen flat. The drains may be better, but the environment is just as squalid: and we have got Subtopia instead of Town and Country, into the bargain.

There are two elements: eating away in the centre and dumping down at the fringe. The second is illustrated by council housing, not private housing, because the council ought to have known better, and because it is local planning, which ought to be reversing the trend, that is actually encouraging it. The leaders of planning – a long way up from the insides of the local offices that reject modern houses as being out of tone with the amenities of the (speculative semi-det) district – recognise the futility of it, but they have backed the wrong horse; decrying increased urban densities in the heart of the town, when that is the only thing likely to save us, and proposing new and expanded towns when the UK is so small that they will very soon all run together.

The creation of fragmentation public parks, as at Lancaster, is pointless (*Lancaster*, of all places, with the only urbane streets between Manchester and the Border); the amenity is negligible and the loss to the town enormous. Buildings must be replaced by buildings, but not as ramshackle and visually careless as the example in Carlisle, overleaf. Otherwise, the town centre will rot away, and Letchworth is round the corner, not for Garden Cities and New Towns only, but for all the old towns as well.

Anti-urbanism part 1: rot in the centre

This can be diagnosed in four stages:

1. DECAY. Neglected old age causes the decay of pleasant but infirm Georgian buildings in county towns and cottages in villages: nineteenth-century slums in industrial areas become uninhabitable.

Key: 1, Oxford. 2, Blackrod. 3, Kenilworth.

2. DEMOLITION. The offenders are demolished, the area is made into a vacant lot, a hole in the middle of the town. No thought of conversion, no thought of replacement on the site.

Key: 4, Abingdon. 5, Lichfield. 6, Nantwich.

3. SQUATTING. Vehicles move in as buildings move out: privately, as at Warrington 9, or officially at Abingdon, 8.

Key: 7, Oxford. 8, Abingdon. 9, Warrington.

4. SUBSTITUTION. If permanent action is never taken, the hole is made into a public garden or car park, 10 and 11, or rebuilt with temporary buildings breaking the street line, 12.

Key: 10 and 11, Lancaster. 12, Carlisle.

Anti-urbanism part 2: sprawl on the outskirts

... And here is part of what we are offered in exchange for the death of the English town-centre: ten estates in seven counties; and what is there to show in siting or trim that there is any consideration of the genius loci in any of them? – that 5 is a small country town and 4 an outer suburb: or that 3 and 7 are different places at all. However inconvenient it may be for steam-roller planning, sites still have their own natural solutions. There is enough left to suggest that Abingdon, 3, could have been built as tight as possible, in a grid, to prevent sprawl; that at Blackrod, 7, there might have been terraces along the existing street, or closely parallel. Castle Bromwich, 4, eating up Birmingham's green belt, ought never to have been built at all – and still less the speculation now going up opposite the site. Local architects are just pawns in this estate game which is played by the Borough Engineers: if the architect tries to improve, he is soon deflated by footpath and lampstandard. The roads must be made for the houses, and the houses for the site and the county, and not vice versa: and this implies visual control by the architect, not the engineer, not the bye-laws, not the head of the housing committee.

Key: 1, Bletchingdon, Oxon. 2, Newbury. 3, Abingdon. 4, Castle Bromwich. 5, Sandbach. 6, Wigan. 7, Blackrod, Lancs. 8, Bolton-le-Sands, Lancs. 9, Ambleside. 10, Carlisle.

1

2   3   4

5,
6, 7

8, 9,
10

Rural third-degree

If anti-urbanism as applied to an industrial town is a crime, what can one say about the third-degree practised in some rural districts? These examples of the halves of our inevitable equation (decay of the good, replacement by bad) come from the Ploughley RDC, around Bicester, where in ten years one authority has gone a long way towards eradicating what centuries of local building has bestowed and – the worst crime – replacing it by estates that might as well be in Outer Birmingham. The slum drive which is being pursued with the same height-and-sanitation rules, applied blindly, whether the environment is a Salford slum or an Oxon village, will intensify this destruction, as local authorities seem unable to see that they save money if they convert instead of demolishing. England's heritage, going down for the last time, gentlemen!: won't someone see sense, even if it's only for the tourists' dollars?

Key: Old: 1, Charlton on Otmoor. 2, Bucknell. 5, Godington. 6, Finmere. New: 3, Souldern. 4, Oddington. 7, Kirtlington. 8, Bletchingdon.

1, 2,
3, 4

5, 6,
7, 8

The village centre before and after subjection to Subtopian techniques is shown opposite. This has happened to dozens of villages that have become engulfed by urban sprawl: what is much worse is that the same techniques are now being applied to villages in the middle of the country-side – they have become universal.

Below, the surroundings of the Radcliffe Camera as they are and as they might be if it was decided that they ought to be 'improved'. It is obviously absurd, but equivalent absurdities have already happened in the towns opposite. The result is always the same whether it is practised in Oxford or Wigan – the overfurnishing of the outdoor room and the devaluation of the buildings that line it.

Municipal rustic

Municipal Rustic started as the inevitable accompaniment to building splinter Public Parks in the middle of the town, and that was bad enough. It has now become divorced from any amenity. One can sit down or walk around in about one-quarter of these plots: in half of the remainder one can't even get in – they are railed off or on an island. So it is just a matter of applied decoration, and there are no social or economic advantages. Financially, the town can only lose by having them, and the cruellest thing about them is the waste of money, when they are often a council's only concession to the fact that visual standards exist. This is conscious and deliberate Subtopia; wrecking the environment so that man can everywhere see the projection and image of his own humdrum suburban life – mild lusts, mild fears, mild *everything* – a herbaceous border.

Subtopia, as applied to town fringes, came first, for Municipal Rustic is very nearly a post-war disease. This, then, is the second orbit of the downward spiral, the result of one generation having lived in limbo. The psychological chain by which it becomes the standard solution is worth tracing, because its pattern of phobia and nostalgia is not only a mess, it is *the* mess: the same pattern that produces fear of not getting on, or not keeping up with the neighbours, mixed with vicarious longings for a better world, projected through TV stars or the pools. When urban improvements are mooted, the official concerned gets an automatic reflex against urban forms and in favour of rural ones, the legacy of our squalid nineteenth-century urban life. But the only rural forms he knows are suburban ones, and in a rush of nostalgia he translates his architectural equivalents of rustic gnomes and Devon pixies into the town centre, unable to see the difference. The result is neither town nor country – Subtopia.

Municipal Rustic is wrong because it replaces large scale by small scale – grass and trees by snippets of flowerbeds 5, dainty walls 4, coy fencing, 8 and 9.

It is wrong because it confuses private and public, 2 and 9 – the flower garden is an admirable thing as a personal possession, but its significance is that it is personal.

It is wrong because it blurs distinctions – between country and town 13, between car park and street 8, even between one half of the town and another 6, where to convert an exciting change of level into an enlarged rockery needs a keen eye for the possibility of creating mediocrity.

It is wrong because it doesn't act as a foil, the basic reason why greenery should be in the town at all. For one thing, most of the year it isn't green, just grubbed up soil and blackened shrubs, 13. The surroundings are crowded: the plots answer with high density art work. The traffic is bustling: the plots echo it in their fussy treatment. This is extension of the jungle, not amelioration.

It is wrong because, as the sum of all these things, it blows open the town, destroying the old relation of buildings, people and space and replacing it by . . . what? By nothing definable, and that is just the point: it is the gaseous pink marshmallow mentioned in the Introduction. These twenty views have stopped being urban scenes altogether, and become Subtopia.

Key: 1, Andover. 2, Newbury. 3, Abingdon. 4, Oxford. 5, Woodstock. 6, Chipping Norton. 7, Leamington. 8, Newcastle under Lyme. 9, Rugeley. 10, Nantwich. 11, Leigh. 12, Chorley. 13 and 14, Lancaster. 15, Bowness-on-Windermere. 16, Carlisle.

1, 2,
3, 4

5, 6,
7, 8

9, 10,
11, 12

13, 14,
15, 16

Advertising stations

Beautifying in even sharper relief: planned-for and legislated-for attempts at reducing the impact of Horrid Commerce. The attempt to art them up is ten times worse than anything that Horrid Commerce can do. The worst thing about Northwich, 9, is the coy drystone walls and blushing shrubs in front: and at Lancaster, 8, the basic fault is a combination of the planning that caused the site to be a hole in the town and the planning that made the railed-off garden in the name of amenity. The *Review* wants not less advertising but more: neater, crisper and less standardised (*AR*, November, 1951), made free of the walls from which planning, in the name of Good Taste, is trying to drive it. It would transform the perspective of the end walls of semi-detacheds, for example – but is it likely?

Key: 1, Southampton. 2–4, Longton. 5, Newcastle-under-Lyme. 6 and 9, Northwich. 7, Liverpool. 8, Lancaster.

Rural municipal rustic

From gardening the roundabout in the city centre, it is only too easy to do the same thing to the road trim on the by-pass, and then to extend it along that newly-built double carriageway. This is Municipal Rustic put back in the country, and shown up all the more because the small-scale planting and fussy design is seen against the genuinely rural rhythms which are neither small scale nor fussy. It is another reminder that the style is *Rustic* not *Rural*; the conception of the country has been modified psychologically and physically to fit a suburban back garden. It is an admirable microcosm in a suburban back garden, but it won't transplant.

If the administrative fault behind this is cleared up, the visual offence would probably disappear. The planting should have been decided by trained landscape architects when the road was cut or the roundabout made. Instead, it has been left to the local authorities, and while this might have been an admirable thing in the 1500's or 1830's, it is disastrous in the 1950's. If you doubt it, look at the results: scratchings in the turf, 2, 6, 8 – one of them with its attached reward – and carefully nurtured conifers, 4, that will never look anything more than dowdy poor relations of the oaks and elms in the hedgerows. Roundabouts in particular incite misapplied fantasy, like the concrete path neatly laid out for those who walk in the middle of the road, 5. And when what was obviously designed in two dimensions is translated into three, 1 and 3, the results are startling: a Le Nôtre layout applied to a Repton hill all seen through the wrong end of a telescope.

Planting may need to be camouflage it could often be a large-scale setting, like that the Enclosure Commissioners provided – big hedges, big borders and a clean roadside; and in some cases it should not be there at all – road and landscape impinging directly. None of these cases is ever likely to be carried out under the present method of Beautifying by the local authority with a segment of the rates. This must always be a kind of advertisement hoarding: 'Look, we are spending your money wisely, we have dug a little plot, isn't it nice?'

So it may be, in vacuo or behind the bandstand; but not out in the middle of Oxon, Warwicks, Staffs, Cheshire or Lancs.

Key: 1, Oxford By-pass. 2, A34, Yarnton, Oxon. 3, A34 near Woodstock. 4, A446, Coleshill. 5, A34, Trentham. 6, Northwich By-pass. 7, Warrington. 8, A57, Barton-on-Irwell, Lancs. 9, A580 near Leigh. 10, A6, Bamber Bridge, Lancs.

1, 2,
3, 4

5, 6,
7

8, 9,
10

Standard fringes

Here is the guessing game. It is enough justification for a special issue were there nothing else to complain about on the whole route. Romsey, Oxford, Stratford, Birmingham, Stafford, Newcastle-under-Lyme, Northwich, Warrington and Bolton-le-Sands are shown here jumbled up; not in south-to-north order as the other sets have been. Which *is* which?

Everything has been said elsewhere in the issue about the visual and consequent social evil of this ring of Subtopia that girdles every English town. There is no point in repeating the arguments, and the photographs, unhappily, can speak for themselves. This is murder we are committing: first of our surroundings, then, as they react on us, of ourselves. If you say that to alter it is impracticable, uneconomic and unrealistic, remember that a nation-wide organisation to track down physical murder is just as impracticable, uneconomic and unrealistic on the face of it, yet we have the CID. The obstacles will disappear if we want them to, and the first stage towards that is awareness. This issue, condensed, says Look Out: This is Awful.

Key: 1, Stratford. 2, Warrington. 3, Northwich. 4, Stafford. 5, Newcastle-under-Lyme. 6, Oxford. 7, Romsey. 8, Bolton-le-Sands, Lancs. 9, Birmingham.

1, 2, 3

4, 5,
6,

7, 8,
9

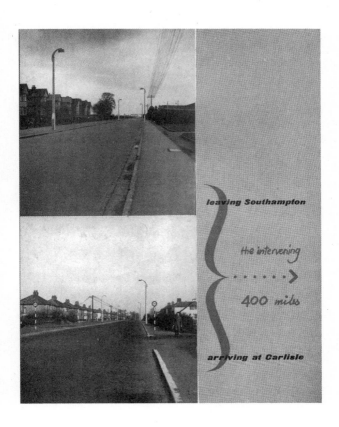

leaving Southampton

the intervening

· · · · · · >

400 miles

arriving at Carlisle

47

Subtopia Chart and Route Map

The grey line within the grey band shows the route; the light grey band
shows the approximate area from which outrages have been selected.
The dark grey areas are those which can be considered the main centres
of expanding Subtopia.
The black lines are trunk roads.

– Route Book –

T he Route Book really needs no introduction:
plan and intention of the next forty-five pages
are painfully self evident. It may claim the doubtful
distinction of being the first example of a travel agent's
trip in reverse – picking out the bad, not the good – that
has been carried through from one end of the country
to the other and has not just picked on selected black
spots. In fact it is only since 1939 that such a thing has
been possible. That is one of the points made by the
map opposite; the dark grey Subtopian areas (approximately done, but they give a good general idea) are at
first glance just a restatement of population density.
A closer look shows, besides the bloated sizes of the
towns themselves, splinter groups spreading over the
whole country, representing airfields, wholesale afforestation, military camps, wire jungles and 'out-county'
estates. The map has caught the precise moment where
it has begun to run together – whence our definition
of Subtopia as the extension to the whole land surface
of the mess that has already been made of the edges of
our towns.

Point two to come from the map is that the route
really is a fair cross-section: neither the best nor the

worst but half of each. Lakeland was added as a deviation from the rigid north-south line to bring in an area which is supposed to be a National Park and show that the disease is just as rampant there too. The route takes in approximately thirty miles per page, and this means that only a limited number of outrages can be shown (those left over would make another Route Book). It also means that mid-Oxon gets the same coverage as industrial Staffs; the result proves unanswerably that Subtopia is already all round us.

The first stage towards doing something is to know what is wrong. Some of the things in the route may seem trivial, and to mention them may seem to be shouting about objects that can be taken for granted and assimilated by the eye, as railways have been. The point of that is to try and get rid of the habit of taking for granted, because above a certain density it ceases to work – with the railways, in Swindon goods yards, for example – and we are getting near that density now. Try this way of seeing things on some part of your holiday route this year. Before long you find yourself becoming incredibly angry; and when sufficient people become sufficiently angry, that will be the end of Subtopia.

SOUTHAMPTON – WHITCHURCH

Subtopia breaks the traveller in gently: on leaving
Southampton, the Winchester road is a leafy parkway
passing from the centre of the town to the country, 1 –
a phenomenon achieved by a long thin common which
hides the miles of suburbs on either side. No other
town on the route will be so fortunate – but even here
the illusion is blurred with concrete lamp-standards.
Further out one realises that the fundamental fact
about the English scene is that most of it is crammed
to bursting with private houses. There are just too
many people chasing too few green fields. The triangle
between Winchester, Southampton and Portsmouth
is like this: so how inept to erect a post-war transformer station and its progeny of sleazy wires in one
of the few pieces of green countryside, 2 and 3, south
of Chandlers Ford. Following them west, one comes
to their source, 4, a wire jungle in the middle of the

1   2   3   4

5   6   7   8

country. Farther north, one of many little huts squats by the roadside, 5. It can stand for the whole band of Things in Fields – so many different uses resulting in such monotonous, similar buildings – a gabled roof, attempted resemblance to a small cottage, a firm boundary of wire, and an air of having been dropped from a great height. And opposite this are huts left over from a wartime camp, 6: what couldn't be helped but should be moved facing what can't be moved but should have been well designed. The Winchester By-Pass, 7 and 8, has prevented the city being battered without mercy, like St. Albans, and is a relatively gentle introduction to England's steam-roller roads. The centre planting is seen in two stages: rose-border in 7 and jungle in 8, both inappropriate. The jungle is an attempt at illusion, but it doesn't come off: cars peep through like lions and tigers in the Douanier Rousseau prototype; and reference to the other side of the road makes the absurdity complete – a bad illusion is worse than none at all.

Going north out of Winchester there is what looks like a small oilfield on the left, 9: a look at the map would show that it was, in fact, Crawley W.T. Station.

Towards it the *Review* is taking the unhelpful but justifiable attitude – 'this is a horrid mess: what can be
done about it?' The excuse of 'But there must be . . .
airfields, grid lines and wireless masts . . .' is a conveni-
ent cover for lack of any attempt to control them.

Next, two small Hampshire towns with comple-
mentary problems: Whitchurch, 11, has traffic trouble but no wire, Stockbridge, 10, has wire but no
traffic problem – being largely a coaching town the
main street was tailored to fit: with such success that
it is wide enough to take to-day's traffic comfortably.
Houses are small scale in relation to the road, but the
important thing is that they are *in relation* to the road,
not thrown alongside it with mutual loathing like the
ribbon-development south of Birmingham, on page

80. It is a compromise, not a war between steam-roller road and aloof houses, and this makes the wire all the more noticeable – with no thought of compromise at all, shouting 'this is a Main Road not a High Street.' Like the lamp-standards in Warwick High Street, it destroys the space enclosed by the street and the buildings, a space as real as any internal space: it is equivalent, say, to stringing up clothes-lines inside St. Paul's.

At Whitchurch the problem is pathetically simple – two main roads, meeting head-on in the middle of the small town. Make an arid roundabout where the town focus should be and traffic can go through it thicker and faster – vortex instead of focus, nailing Whitchurch securely to its cross of asphalt.

WHITCHURCH – ABINGDON

South of Newbury, at the newly enlarged American air-field at Greenham Common, there is an appalling rash of huddled huts on the skyline, 1, and the more subtle ruination created by the by-passes necessary to avoid the two-mile runway, and the extra area enclosed by wire for security's sake. There is no point in questioning the necessity; unhappily it is as necessary as coal mines or arterial roads. But one can ask two things: whether the siting was reasonable, and whether any attempt was made to respect the surroundings. As to the first, arguments could be advanced against any site in Britain; but even so, Greenham Common is on a ridge top, visible for miles, and while it didn't use up agricultural land it meant the loss of ten square miles of open common; the new form of an old battle – Enclosure. The surroundings obviously were not thought of at all – either by camouflage, which has obvious advantages or by making the airfield a crisp engineering job. Ironically, the refuse from the last war still exists alongside this bulwark against the next; huts from the 1945 use of

Greenham Common, now occupied by squatters, 2: the council has provided, with infallible inappropriateness, a waney-edged privy, 3.

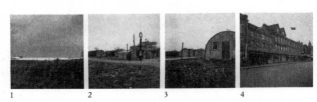

1   2   3   4

Newbury's shopkeepers have an unenviable reputation to keep up, for Newbury has more of its good buildings destroyed by shop fronts than any other town of its size. Especially cruel is the gouging practised in 4, which has spoilt not one house but five. Nor have the public authorities lagged behind: at the junction of A34 and the Bath Road there is a beautified plot, 6. There *was* a Gothick toll house. Older readers may remember it, for this is how it appeared in 1939, 5, when the *Review* protested against the proposed demolition – the ideal 'before and after' photograph, nor-

5   6

mally so hard to obtain after the event. A handsome building and an impressive roadscape effect (shuttling off the traveller to Bath or Oxford) have been replaced by a piece of Subtopia. Of course, it would be demolished for road widening; the road is as narrow as ever, the corner is as acute – the plots and paving even occupy exactly the same site.

The Berkshire Downs are the end of the chalk country and of Southern England: you get to the top and see before you Harwell, 7 and 8, stretched out like a slug in the foreground. The siting has made it an almost impossible problem; on a step halfway up the downs so that everything is presented to the surrounding countryside on a plate, and this had no justification – any aerodrome in Britain would have done as well. The apologium of Sir John Cockcroft has been quoted before (in Murray's guide to Berkshire) but it is worth repeating: 'a start had to be made quickly, and the only solution was to provide prefabs and to erect them on our own site where services and sewers were available and where the minimum of consent had to be obtained'. The old Litany of Expediency.

7   8

The Vale of White Horse is the vale of orchards and military dumps. The RAF created Harwell, the Ministry of Supply enlarged it – to complete the round of the Services, here is an Army dump at Steventon, 9, and a Navy dump at Grove, 10. We have become so used to wartime expedients that we have not noticed how they have quietly become peacetime fixtures, or just how much of England has been swallowed up by these parks of obsolescent equipment.

9

10

LAND GRAB

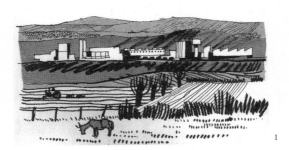

Views from the two great escarpments of Southern
England – chalk and limestone: Harwell from the
Berkshire Downs, 1, and Kineton Ordnance Depot
from Sun-rising Hill, near Banbury, 2. Both are expedients that have become permanent – Harwell from the
pre-war RAF expansion, Kineton from the build-up of
stores before D-Day; both absorb good agricultural
land, both extend the limbo of unplanned technology a little further into a countryside where it has no
place. Both, from their siting, employ land-grab in

another more subtle way – they poison the whole view. There is no liberation in a forty-mile prospect which has an atom factory in the middle foreground, and this isn't just an æsthetic quibble, it stems from a primary human need, that of being able to experience a natural order in which there is no dominant human accent. A well-designed atom factory would give the noble view, but not the liberation: there is a place for both in the environment if there is room for both, but – the inevitable density clause – in England *every* view will soon have its industrial or military installation, and most of them badly designed as well.

Principles can only protect the unspoilt; these two are here, *faits accomplis*: what can be done about them? Basically two things, dramatisation and camouflage, and the sites split neatly. Harwell is a fixture, so big and so prominent that camouflage would give a greater jolt than the atom factory is at present; letting modern industrial forms express themselves clearly is the only solution, which is what the MOW's new buildings are doing. Kineton is just a mess – and is it a justifiable mess? Are we going to attack France to-morrow, or is it dispersed enough from the H-bomb which would obliterate Birmingham, only thirty miles away? If it is essential it ought to be camouflaged, which is surely a military advantage as well.

(The drawings are improvisations on the basic theme of the actual forms for security's sake, but they have the same visual weight as the real thing.)

ABINGDON – CHIPPING NORTON

In this section the process of false arterial road-making can be studied as a gradual growth. 1 shows the process just beginning, with a concrete footpath; soon everything splits up like amoebae – two footpaths, two cycle tracks, two carriageways; the cycle tracks themselves wide enough to be a reasonable lane, a feature pointed by 3. And in 2, the planting scratched on the surface, only heightens the arid effect. 4–6 are exam-

ples of the dumping of public utilities which unobtrusively accompanies their schemes, a nibbling process which reaches a certain density unnoticed and then transforms the countryside or village into a background for ill-sited and carelessly designed pieces of apparatus: Subtopia again. 4, with its curt announcement, is a part of 5, a prefabricated cuckoo in a nest of wire. The footpath is indeed closed, and the way of announcing it shows Authority – and Authority without taste – in its most sinister aspect. The difference between 'This footpath is closed', 'No loitering', and 'This view is forbidden' or 'Do not think about this building' is only one of degree not of kind. 6, just south of Blenheim, is part of the small-change of technology which can be seen up and down the country.

Woodstock has been dealt with before (AR, December, 1951, page 380): one of the most imposing towns of its size in Britain, with the cruellest-sited domestic grid in Britain. Why do Englishmen who would become violently indignant if they saw a mesh of wire over the National Gallery's Gainsboroughs and Wilsons remain quite content to see comparable

7   8   9

works of architecture through an engineer-imposed graticule? There would be only one thing that could sap the town's individuality any further, and here it is, 7 and 8: one of the pylons made into a plot, with little shrubs, a little seat and flower baskets halfway up. This is purely in the Victorian tradition of putting pants on piano legs: as futile and as silly; by comparison the footwear of the unimproved pylon is full of sturdy elegance. Everything in present-day life tends to standardise surroundings and blur the separateness of town, village and country: it is vital that public amenities shouldn't confuse the scene further by bringing a fragment of municipal park or front garden into the town centre. On the way out the grid ends its way through the town in a tangle of wire, pole, pylon, cut-down tree and sand tip, 9.

OXFORD

Coming from Abingdon the first sight of Oxford will probably be from the foot of Boar's Hill, 1. It is typical of the whole problem, a magnificent skyline framed between concrete lamp standards, and with a foreground of pylons, railways and allotments. One longs for something that could cut across the random system by which changes are made in Britain's appearance and persuade, for example, the Oxford City Council to co-operate with British Railways to make over the money they use in laying out ornamental gardens to the Forestry Commission, who could plant trees to mask the foreground; to get someone from the Ministry of Transport (and the Berks C.C.?) to clear up the island, or at least make it consistent, and replace the lamp standards. This multiplicity is a basic problem: that each of these bodies has a different end

in view, which is not visual, and that the visual case is only stated in opposition – by private individuals, or the CPRE – and not by co-operation. Planning, which was supposed to deal with it, has been castrated because it has no positive visual code but only negative non-visual rules. In the city centre there are conflicting and disconcerting impressions, and the most evident is likely to be the traffic round Carfax, 2: a system that required widening in the 1790's to provide for stage coaches now carries through north-south traffic and supports a 30,000 industrial population that should never have been sited there at all. There can be no question of widening now; and the only solution when the old plan and modern traffic are as irreconcilable as they are here is a partial or complete ban on vehicles in the centre. The false rural Cotswold tradition in architecture – false because applied to the most truly urban city in England (plus fours with an Anthony Eden hat) – exemplified by Nuffield College has been carried into the whole environment in the form of ornamental gardens, both by City and University: in the main street, 3, in Nuffield 'quad' itself, 4, and in Hertford College, 5, where measures have been taken to prevent the lawn from flying away by sticking it down at the corners like a photograph. And look at the same idea, 300 miles away, at the gardens at Carlisle, 6. One doesn't know which would be the more piqued, Hertford College or Carlisle City Council, at the idea that they shared identical bad taste, but it is true. The city has its own ways of upsetting the urban pattern. The view of the Clarendon building down Broad Street is dominated by a particularly inappropriate car park attendant's hut, 7, and the approach to Magdalen Tower from the east is dominated by a dowdy plot and shelter, 8.

5   6   7   8

Oxford is the perfect place to study rehousing because it had no bomb damage at all, so that one could expect to find a model essay in preventing sprawl and careful design. What it has got, in fact, is decaying houses in the centre, 9, condemned years ago and remaining condemned without a thought of conversion; and a huge post-war estate beyond the by-pass, in the middle of the countryside, that is a

9   10   11   12

promising candidate for the most dreary in the whole country, whether in siting, skyline, 10, or detail, 11. The typical outlook of local planning to modern techniques is shown in the treatment of the BISF Gibberd houses; these were designed in the expectation that an informal and broken layout would be used, and bright colours to diversify the effect. What has happened? – rule of thumb has set them down in rows one after another like by-pass Tudor and then painted them all cream with cosy green trim to the doors and windows, 12. In designing them, Gibberd made the best of a difficult task; Oxford City Council have made the worst of an easy one.

The tour finishes with two photographs that convey some of the savage humour in extremes of inappropriateness that makes Oxford read like an extra chapter of Gulliver's Travels. The Oxford gasworks, 1 (overleaf), was an appalling blunder of siting in the 1890s and remains so to-day – yet 60 years of it did not prevent the City from contemplating an extension after the war, and after the Oxford Plan had specifically recommended resiting, which was only stopped with immense effort. The *jeu d'esprit* of 2 is not a glade in the New Forest, but the top of a roundabout on the Oxford by-pass, Oxford's parting gesture to the north-bound tourist, the wrong thing in the wrong place. It overlooks streets full of inter-war semi-detacheds, and a few vacant sites where post-war semi-detacheds are being put up in the same style.

1

2

BICESTER GARRISON

Bicester Garrison: Five miles of it on your car speedometer, ringed with wire and full of 'keep-out' notices … Keep out … Keep out … Dogs patrol at night, 3. The centre is a little hill which has been completely covered with huts, 4, and this is visible for miles in the flat country around – the area it poisons is more like forty square miles. We have become conditioned to large areas of the country being given over to military use – Aldershot and Salisbury Plain, for instance – nor can one dispute the necessity for dispersal; but when one of the Services makes an assault on fresh country, two things can be asked of it – that it attempts camouflage and that it tidies up as it goes along. Planting – even conifer planting – would make an immense difference to Graven Hill. Is it impossible to ask the Government departments

to co-operate, and at the same time prevent more square miles elsewhere being eaten up by conifers? In any case there is no excuse for the dereliction of 5 and 6. The Gun Park, 7, raises a third point – it is three miles from the main depot and there are many other installations at a similar distance. Dispersal must stop somewhere, there must be a compromise between the need to be secure against attack and the need to prevent the whole country being overrun with dumps and camps. It is no use being prepared if in the process you destroy what you are supposed to defend, and the English countryside, equally remote from collective or prairie farm, is a very special part of that heritage.

CHIPPING NORTON – WARWICK

At Chipping Norton, the end of one of the main streets is no place for a transformer station, 1, while the 1939–45 war memorial is a perfect example of Adding the Art to a basically inoffensive design. One can see it growing visibly more 'artistic' as one starts close to the tablet and then walks backward, accumulating each plot and shrub, 2. Appallingly genteel gates complete the effect, 3. The Rollright Stones, 4–6, enjoy the unspoilt surroundings which are essential if pre-Roman monuments are to be significant evocations of history rather than a number in an archæological catalogue (the northward view, for instance, is a 400 ft. drop to 20 miles of South Warwickshire, rather than a

1   2   3

4

5

6

military camp at twelve o'clock, eight hundred yards, as at Stonehenge). However, the MOW have tried hard to break the continuity: by attrition on the circle, 4, with railings and notices, and by brute force on the King's Stone, with the incredible result shown in 5 and 6, capped by an observer post right on the skyline. The result is complete disenchantment; the shock and the philosophical implication of yesterday-in-today have been guide-booked into an Historical Attraction, something to be looked at pedantically and individually and not seen whole as part of the landscape. Art has admittedly had the last laugh, for now the King's Stone has unconsciously reproduced the pattern of strain and confinement that modern sculptors have been trying to convey deliberately. It could be the Unknown Bureaucratic Prisoner: but the gain is less than the loss.

South Warwickshire really merits its reputation, the farthest north where you can see a landscape gay without any reservations. This makes its few blemishes all the more of a shock, such as this ruinously sited transformer station near Tredington, 7, on top of an isolated hill, breaking the back of views both towards and away from it. 8 is an aspect of Stratford the tourist posters don't mention: Stratford aerodrome, disused but not cleared up. Caravans for sale, 9 – north of Stratford. Again, diagrams of progress which have arrived in the landscape without any question. Like charabancs in the Lakes, they are inevitable – though they don't leave at 6 p.m. – yet they can ruin any scene in which they are sited. 10 and 11 come near Wellesbourne – a pylon and hut that are rude to the

7 8 9

10, 11

GOVERNMENT PROPERTY
ANY UNAUTHORISED PERSONS
INTERFERING OR TRESPASSING
WILL BE PROSECUTED

landscape and a notice that is rude to the passer-by. As at Kidlington, the offence is against good manners as well as good taste, a sinister parallel.

STRATFORD & HENLEY-IN-ARDEN

Stratford and
Henley-in-Arden

1   2

Two towns, included because they show the spread of
bogus historicism, a kind of retrospective Subtopia. It
is history made easy, or rather history made cosy (no
bad drains or squalor), and it is what the majority of
people look for, whether they are British or foreign
tourists. This attitude tends to concentrate, luckily, on
a very few national figures and places, and Stratford is
one of them. Just as Salisbury Plain is considered a lost
cause to the Army, so Stratford can be regarded as a
hostage to Tourism; its existence is the guarantee that
Warwick or Alcester or Leamington shall stay a little
less spoiled. The external and internal manifestations
are the rows of motor-buses and mock half-timbered
house, 1 and 2: people come with olde worlde preconceptions, expecting to have them confirmed, so naturally Stratford sees to it that they are confirmed. It is all
part of Subtopia; the quite legitimate urge to put your
past on show leads to faking on lines that wouldn't
matter in Hollywood but in Stratford undermine what

3   4

5   6

is genuine. That's the trouble with bogus medievalism or even bogus Georgian – for people of any discrimination they devalue the real thing.

The town is full of significant details such as the rustique huts for car-park attendant, 3, and man-park attendants, 4, and the maze of rose-gardening by the river bank, 5.

The attitude can be seen spreading outside the tourist limits, first in Beautification by the Gas Board, 6 (again, no attempt to design the huts beyond, only a hurried and ineffective screen of camouflage around the gates) and then to Henley-in-Arden, five miles north on the Birmingham road. It can show most shades of falsification from the Birmingham suburb nailed-on of 7 to the much more vicious arting-up of

8 and 9. With what care have the Tudor features been encouraged to make the street genteel and false. How lovingly has Georgian brickwork been made to sprout a bow window, coyly leaded, in its bowels. As has been said, Stratford is only tolerable as a guarantor of the peace of the surrounding district; as the leader of a Stratford School it is a menace.

WARWICK – N. BIRMINGHAM

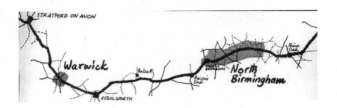

Warwick's High Street has only one thing wrong with it – apart from the main road traffic that steam-rollers through it – 25 ft. lamp standards carrying 6 ft. lamps, 1. Ugly anywhere, especially cruel here, where the whole virtue of the street is the repetition of similar rectilinear relations on a much smaller scale in Georgian wall and window patterns. To ape this on a gigantic scale and using a third dimension, cutting into the street space, not running along it, is about as insensitive a treatment as could have been devised. At the north end there is a medieval gate: heavily preserved (lucky for its Gothick superstructure!), traffic squeezes round its right flank, 2. The archway thus left, instead of being used as a footway, is completely blocked by the silliest flowerbed in the whole journey, 3 and 4:

1   2   3   4

the pedestrians meanwhile form a human sandwich between coach and masonry, making the traffic block even more acute.

Leamington has another tale of lamp standards: and the careful choice of the wrong lamp standards for the wrong place shows some ingenuity. Warwick has a small repeating pattern and the lamp standards give it elephantiasis: Leamington is full of long stucco sweeps, so the standards stick in the middle and punch holes in them, changing the skyline from cornice to trough and keyhole, 5 and 6. 7 is a little reminder of motor trim skyline at Kenilworth.

8 is the view down Coleshill High Street, with the point that Hams Hall power station in the distance makes a fine contrast only if the space in between is green, not smudged with a big council estate. In fact, in the circumstances, it should not have been there at all, 9 (on the previous page); this green belt, sandwiched between Coventry and the Black Country, is too small, and has to serve too many people to be eroded like this. Sharawaggi can only be practical if the environment as a whole is sane; a Gothick ruin premised the big Palladian park around it.

On the fringes of Birmingham: planning gone pur-
blind – a ribbon of newly-built spec, houses stretching
out into the diminished countryside. 'Stop them? Certainly not, they are perfectly in keeping with the landscape' – there is a pre-war ribbon on the other side of
the road. If this is anyone's ideal, 10 and 11, it is a very
mediocre one – and that is the definition of Subtopia
all over again.

SUPERIMPOSED PATTERNS

Studies in superimposed patterns near Birmingham: left, spec. building newly erected behind a screen of mature trees typical of Warwickshire, 1; right, the fortuitous effect of superimposing two Subtopian patterns one on another – spec. building and grid wires – along the same stretch of A452, 2: a sharp contrast from two elements, although both blur the landscape. Opposite, the sharp, clean and impressive contrast of countryside and industry being themselves, except that it is in the middle of the thin green strip between Birmingham and Coventry, 3.

1   2

There might almost be a solution here to transmute urban sprawl. The first represents what must not go any further, what planning should have prevented any way – an unrestrained herd stampede into the countryside. The second is a possible treatment of every town's penumbra, as a multiplication of savage jokes like this. The third is what we can't afford, as we are on too small an island that is too densely populated and too densely industrialised. So if our town edges are already a chaos of discordant elements, why not order them by intensification, not camouflage? More industry, housing and wire, not less, to give a ring separating town and countryside. This part of Subtopia can't be removed and it can't be camouflaged. Why not make the best of a bad job, and play its constituents against each other — the indifference of wires, lamp-standards and factories against the ædicules of innumerable detached houses and the primness of municipal rustic, with the proviso, of course, that Town and Country remain unspoilt inside and beyond the iron ring.

3

N. BIRMINGHAM – STAFFORD

How can one blame the private builders, when the best that the Corporation could do in making a neighbourhood centre is shown at Kingstanding? An immense rond-point, 1, has wide avenues, 100ft. or more, galloping off into the distance, lined with semi-detached houses that cannot look anything else but dwarfed. The corner sites are accented with buildings like 2, making a timid site even more mousey – and the centre is a huge roundabout, with its quota of signs, flower-bedded and railed in. The middle of the 'town' is completely sterile – people can't get there, being cut off by traffic, and there is nowhere for them to go when they do. And here is the King's Standing itself, 3, the point where Charles I is supposed to have watched a minor Civil War engagement, in the middle of a sterilised – ploughed up, in fact – strip, one of the avenues of this compass rose, vigorously fenced. The effect rebounds straight back on to the mean-spirited surroundings, the idea that the environment can be parcelled up – that is a Historical Exhibit, this is a Recreation Area, there is a Beauty Spot – while the ground in between is just forgotten. Men are much more efficient machines when their activities *are* parcelled up like this, as productivity experts and dictators, Left and Right, have found out – they just stop being complete men, that's all.

1   2   3   4

4 is a roadside quarry near Brownhills: perfectly legitimate, but it should make some attempt to tidy up. 5 is the same thing in public terms north of Wolverhampton: little else can be said that hadn't been mentioned about the other installations – the point is just the cumulative effect. 6 comes from a Ministry of Supply depot at Featherstone – in the middle of the country, with no attempt made to clear up the wartime mess, except possibly to renew the wire; a little more ground

5   6

eaten up both physically, from the farmers, and figuratively, from the eyes of the people in the overcrowded Black Country who have to fan out further to get away from nineteenth-century industrialisation and – far more widespread – twentieth-century Subtopia.

Penkridge, 7–9, was a large village west of Cannock until a few years ago. Now it is backcloth to a grotesque combination – floral dance that is Totentanz as well. The roundabout eases nobody's problem, 7, for the traffic coming down the side road from Cannock is negligible. Plant little shrubs ringed with asphalt, instead of an open space, and the corollaries of selling your village to The Road have already appeared – a hoarding to frame the church, 9, and a badly-sited filling station, 8. The ensemble depresses one more community which had a spirit of its own into an echo of the Coventry By-Pass.

7   8

9

Cannock Chase is the first introduction that this route provides to the work of the Forestry Commission. Cannock Chase was an open space, and a much-needed one, just north of a crowded mining area: some of it still is, 11: comparison with 10, taken on the other side of the road, shows how ugly the transformation is. For the sake of a few less pit props, the site could have been landscaped properly and proper paths provided, not the Gothick Horror of 10.

10   11

STAFFORD – SANDBACH

The main street of Stafford is crowded and narrow, but it had just one open space in front of the Town Hall; this has been destroyed by converting it into a garden. To halve the previous breathing area with flower beds is very silly – why not leave it open and let people stop instead of being harried between plot and bus queue, 1? The concrete post is best described by that out of date but useful word 'debased', 3, and if you are possessed of an elegant eighteenth-century Town Hall, it is an odd thing to try to discredit it with fussy ironwork and window boxes of bark, 2 and 4 – even if you do wish it were half timbered.

Meaford Power Station, 5, is far from being Neo-Technic, but that is not our present concern. What is germane is the entirely mid-twentieth-century wire, sterilising the land behind and winding its serpentine way right over the horizon. What is the point of that, apart from sheer callousness? If the plant must be protected it can surely be done closer than this. 6 is a mess near Eccleshall, 7 and 8 show a perversion of concrete that is more irritating than usual, with the lumpish arm rests and genteel quirk of the panel below them. From the inscription it was obviously put up with the best of intentions, such things always are, and there was probably nothing better to choose from, a fact which implies a lack of taste in the manufacturer as well as the buyer.

5   6   7   8

Cheshire is full of little towns, canals and small factories, and it digests them very well. One of the few areas on the whole of this route where industry and nature augment each other is near Middlewich, where the factories provide the punctuation that the landscape needs, and the fields set off the crisp industrial rhythms. Crisp is the operative word; the division is sharp: exhilarating, not enervating. However, there are still two sources of visual offence for Cheshire – municipal improvements in the towns and Government departments in the country. Here is an example of each: a dump of signs and symbols in the centre of Nantwich where there should have been a positive statement of urbanity, 9; and beyond it three studies of decay from Cheshire's own Les Baux, 10-12, Calveley airfield. As the notice points out, the Ministry of Works disclaims any responsibility for damage due to trespass on the derelict buildings – what a terrible example of ministerial couldn't care less. Whose fault is it that the buildings weren't pulled down and the land returned years ago? These derelict camps can be paralleled by the hundreds up and down the country, and when they have reached this stage it can't be pleaded that they might be required in a future war (and whoever got anywhere by living from war to war?). To make these usable again would cost as much as erecting new buildings so why not remove them?

SANDBACH – WARRINGTON

The other half of Cheshire is unspoilt even though it is nibbled on the north by Lancashire overspill – for example this new private estate in embryo in the middle of the vital Green Belt between Knutsford and Manchester, 1 (see overleaf; which Manchester Corporation is also trying to demolish, with their proposals for a satellite at Mobberley). The rest of the county does manage the incredible fragile co-existence of industry and rurality – the eye takes in the factory on the skyline, but doesn't worry about it. It is partly clean edges, and partly the stark rectilinear pattern of Cheshire's fields and hedges, i.e., it is a special case, and it certainly doesn't happen anywhere else on the route. But it would be a worthwhile factor in planning, when so many industries are quite mobile, to find out on the site which landscapes can 'take it', why, and to what degree.

As was said on pages 89–90, that leaves two main offenders – municipal improvements and government departments. Here they are again (see photos overleaf). The decorated park frontispiece at Northwich,

2, 3, 4, doesn't explode the town but it is a particularly gratuitous bit of Beautification. The park itself is an unspoilt ravine that didn't need tidying up, and the join between natural and stilted is painfully raw. If you want an entrance, keep it light, and if you want amenity, plant seats, not roadside plots with nowhere to stop and sit. Again, at Knutsford, don't plant roadside plots, 5, 6, the simply-designed seats would be far better by themselves. The wire in the background of 6 shows how extra outrages get into the photograph by accident, because there are so many; the whole thing is beginning to coalesce.

As for government departments, there is wire near Middlewich, 7, and wire at Witton, 8: how can so many different combinations all finish up as graceless tangles in one corner of a field? There is the part of RAF Cranage that isn't used, 9, and the whole of RNAS Stretton that is, 10. That takes us to the outskirts of Warrington, where Subtopia comes back with its most

9   10   11

obvious manifestation, the dreary ribbon of private housing, 11. Halfway down it a sign says Buildings for Sale, 12. A housing estate? Then surely it wouldn't be 'buildings', but 'desirable modern residences'. Nor is it, for here are the 'buildings', 13 and 14: huts left over from a wartime camp, being sold to be dispersed and re-erected all over the countryside – like the replaced prefabs – instead of being conserved or demolished. What a reflection on whichever Ministry left the huts to rot – at this stage of dissolution it is difficult to be more precise. In south Cheshire they rot and you are warned that if they kill you it's your own fault; in north Cheshire they rot and you are invited to remove them at your own expense – but either way, they rot, and Authority couldn't care less.

12   13   14

WARRINGTON – PRESTON

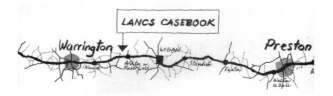

North of Warrington there is thirty miles of England that the guidebooks prefer to talk around. Indefatigable country writers go from half-timbered house to grim fortified manor and usually ignore the fact that between them you have to go past six towns, ten miles of council housing, twenty-five cotton mills and an atom plant. It is not like the Black Country which has limits and visual accents: it was until thirty years ago, but since then urban sprawl has given the last push and created on this route the township of Warrington-Winwick-Ashton-Wigan-Standish-Coppull-Euxton-Bamber-Preston.

The grey uniform desolation, South Lancashire's symphony of wire and asphalt, comes out more clearly in the photographs than words can convey. 1, near Manchester, could be the visual representation of a chapter of Graham Greene; it is an eyesore, but it is not Subtopian. The next pair are part of our substitute for the sky; 2 at Barton and 3 at Leigh.

Lancashire had adopted the swan neck as its lamp-

post, and this misshapen seat, 4 and 5, as the standard fitting in its parks. The silly break in its armrest (this has an obvious affinity with the Stoke-on-Trent school of concrete seats, page 89) peeps out of most villages on the route – these two come from Tarleton and Bolton-le-Sands, photographed in exasperation at the blind acceptance of a poor design off the peg.

6   7   8   9

The trim of the estate at Wigan is very much what could be expected from the distant view, 6, an arid amalgam of concrete and asphalt, hastily modified by rockwork at the main entrance, 7. The visual effect is just as squalid as that of the terraces it replaced in the centre of the town, even though the drains are better. Conversion or replacement on the old site could have improved the drains, lessened the cost, maintained the town centre and left these acres as much needed countryside.

Travelling north out of the industrial range outrages begin to appear in sharper relief – a straightforward brick box but what a surround of concrete and palings, 8: why, when the building itself looks childproof? This is near Blackrod, and so are the swan-neck lamp standards, 9, which impose Uniformity on the few stretches of open country that remain. The sight of these drooping monotonously along a road that is otherwise in the country is far more depressing than any number of industrial streets. Beyond Blackrod there are views to the east of a different landscape, 10, and there are pylons in front to rear up and stamp them with a waspish frame of reference. The photograph is a perfect illustration of the fact that one pylon can,

10   11   12

badly sited, spoil a whole view. There is nothing like an atomic factory for a nice bit of wire, 11, at Euxton, which has sterilised a 50-yard strip of the roadside as well. And Industrial Lancashire ends with a mixed lot of wire, 12, near Blackburn – 'a good general collection', as the stamp dealers say, 'mounted in grass-green album'.

LANCS. CASEBOOK

Up to now, the route has been a linear matter, and the offences have been seen without any historical perspective. Here is an area showing the development chronologically. This square (five by five miles north and east of Warrington) contains only one town, Warrington itself; the acreage built over would still be a small percentage (quite rural, a planner would say, looking at the figures) – yet it is Subtopia. Everything is sited so that it can just be seen from the next camp, or waterworks. The frightening thing is that this twenty-five square miles has been lost to Lancs and England *since 1939*. Before then it was still a buffer; dreary, and with too much industry to be a real relief from St. Helens or Manchester, but *recognisable* country with rhythms of its own. Now Risley atom plant and the spatter of derelict camps north of it have eaten the heart out: Warrington and Leigh have formed fingers – sticky with the marshmallow – diagonally across the area. The series of maps proves it through conscientious revision and the maps themselves manage to reflect the disintegration, subtly. Cartography has become a branch of Subtopia; the environment is starting to get its own back.

1786   1-inch map, B. M. King's Maps, 1865

The matrix. South Lancs developed with isolated farms, not villages, and here they all are. It is the last time that a map can show housing over-scale: to-day's map would be quite black if the area represented by houses were to be enlarged accordingly. The old rhythms can still be glimpsed occasionally to-day – country, field and windbreak, 1 (see overleaf), like the Fylde, farmhouse and windbreak, 2, and the ghost of a better Warrington, 3, typically seen at the end of a street that the nineteenth century made slummy and the twentieth picked holes in. The lesser examples in 4 really will be ghosts – in about six months, by the look of things.

1896   1-inch Ordnance Survey, 2nd edition

The extent of nineteenth-century squalor is shown here, everything from which we reacted so violently and tragically into Town-Country. For 1896, this was industrialised country – we to-day would call it unspoilt. Warrington is still compact, though at the cost of dreary fronts, 5, and drearier backs, 6. This, notice, is a byelaw street. To-day, the bad Industrial Revolution slums have all gone, the gaps they have left are Warrington's canker. They were unconvertible – but these are neither hopeless nor a slum. Conversion could brighten the houses, townscape could transform the street. The way the inhabitants keep the insides – and the doorsteps – would guarantee the rest. Industry was built into the town's growth, together with the housing, 7. It seems a better compromise to have a small terrace

house, a small garden, industry two minutes and the open country five minutes, than a semi-detached house on a huge estate, industry ¾ hour (by bus) and open country nowhere.

In the country there is the railway, 8 (previous page), and hardly anything else. Nearly 1900, with all of Horrid Industrial Lancashire built (things have been improving steadily since, of course), and this plot is still a lung, within walking distance of the towns it serves.

1940   1-inch Ordnance Survey, 6th edition

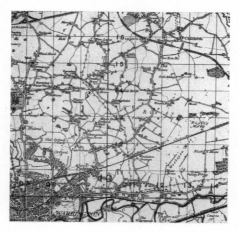

The map begins to look much more familiar but though infections have multiplied the lung is not tubercular yet: and this is, remember, fifteen years ago, not fifty. Warrington has spread out beyond the railway, engulfing Orford with estates like this, 1 (opposite), and private building like this, 2. They replace slum areas in the town centre cleared and left as holes or at best car parks, 3. In the country separate institutions have arrived, all necessary, all hard to argue over – individually. But collectively, one can see from one waterworks, 4 (Houghton Green) to the next (Winwick) 5, and from there to Winwick lunatic asylum, 6.

The pylons have come too, from the approach to the power station, 7, where they are taut and in scale, to the middle of the country, 8, where they are looser

1, 2, 3

4, 5, 6

7, 8

103

and out of scale – and from where one can see both the waterworks and the lunatic asylum. That is the real point, the density of 'casual' installations in a patch of country with towns round the edge.

1952   1-inch Ordnance Survey, 7th edition

To-day's map or rather yesterday's; to-day is a little bit worse, a few more spec. houses and a few more huts, for Subtopia is never static. Warrington has come to explosive decay (see opposite)– a centrifuge at the main cross roads, 9, fragmentation in the open areas, 10, and still more open areas impending, 11. Meanwhile the estates dig further into the country, 12.

9, 10

11, 12

From the edge of building one can now look across and see Winwick lunatic asylum, 1 (see overleaf); and turning the other way the two waterworks and the pylons. In what is left of the country, the old farms are decaying, 2 (see overleaf), while the heart of the lung's tissue has been ripped out by the atomic factory at Risley. Security forbids photographs, but the area on the map tells its own story, appropriately coloured not black but grey. There are also other grey areas in the centre of what was countryside. Mining villages or industrial plant? No – derelict camps, 3–10 (see overleaf), literal sores on the land surface, and not one but half a dozen. Black is now reserved for public buildings – the mental hospital at Winwick is very prominent – and there are two training colleges shown. They turn out to be – two more wartime camps, 11 and 12. Prefabs are re-erected in open country, 13, lamp standards have come to the lanes at Croft, 14, little objects squat by the side of hamlets, 15, each field has its small change of technology, 16. The whole area is lost, forsaken, sold down the line: neither town, country nor suburb, but Subtopia.

And finally the map itself is decaying. That buildings have become represented by grey not black is just a coincidence; but north of Risley there is an old village centre called Culcheth, with a church. Or rather, there was: on our latest edition the name is neatly removed, replaced by the looser anonymous 'Newchurch'. (These old names are outmoded anyway.) And the church? Look back closely and compare with the 1939 map; you will see it marked here as Δ – a triangulation point. How typical that the means of map making should be thought more important than the purpose of the map. 'Come and see our interesting old triangulation point.' Or, again, 'But the church, comrade, it doesn't exist, obviously, it isn't on the map.' A molehill? Certainly, but it will mutate to a mountain using the fatal patent expander of means-not-ends, if we don't look out.

1, 2

PRESTON – LANCASTER

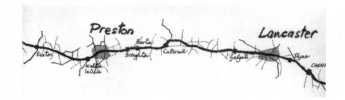

Beyond Preston there is open country at last, and on Sundays industrial south Lancashire becomes over-crowded north Lancashire – these are not main roads but lanes north-east of Garstang, 1, and over the Trough of Bowland, 2. It is an odd idea of relaxation that rushes to a well-known beauty spot and sits ten feet away from another glistening black box in the sun, but it is often the best that can be done, because so much land has been squandered nearer the towns in council estates and semi-detached boxes.

1   2

The rest of the photographs, 3–11 (see opposite and page 110), which epitomise the whole route, come from the Garstang By-Pass, chosen particularly because they are nobody's mess but our own. Garstang (between Lancaster and Preston) is not industrial, and the by-pass was only cut in the 1930s; neither over-crowding nor Ancient Blights can be accepted as an excuse. Broadly speaking, Lancashire is like this, or worse, for forty miles north of Warrington. Again, we can only say where will it all end?

This has a particular moral that was stated by John Piper in 1939: that the fringes of arterial roads should be sterilised, and filling stations and roadhouses gath-ered into nodes every five miles or so. Sixteen years and a war after that, and what have we got? – a planning system that lets worse than ever horrors get through the sieve.

Any one of this nonet could be put into the 'Stand-ard Fringes' at the beginning of this issue, and vice versa: and that is the fundamental crime – removing the identity of a place, not by change, but by imposing

3, 4, 5

6, 7, 8

9   10   11

uniformity. This is the antithesis of real planning. A Dada anti-town planner wanting to obliterate the identity of the world could achieve no more random scatter of elements than this, as though all the houses and fittings in England had been shaken up into a weak solution and then poured over the whole country. Aesthetics apart, it is just plainly anti-social: the people who live there are robbed of the chance of belonging anywhere. They may not wish to use it, but the opportunity should be there just as much as the opportunity for a full education should be available for anyone. To restate as another social analogy: nobody would put up the Gorbals tenements to-day, yet this environment is the spiritual equivalent – where the nineteenth-century slums stunted the body, this twentieth-century Subtopia stunts the mind.

LANCASTER – KENDAL

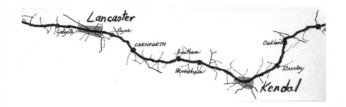

Lancaster, which has some of the most urbane buildings in the North of England, gives a municipal welcome worthy of the least urbane suburban satellite. If it is Harrison of Chester's masterpiece, it is also the city of small rustic plots, 1–4. 1 is near the Castle, 2–4 are in the centre, four different ways of prostituting streets. That they are put up in good faith only makes the task of opposing them harder, because it seems impossible to make people see, before it is too late, that 'town' is not 'country'.

2, 3

1 4

A6 north out of Lancaster is the overture to a different landscape, to the mountains which will now never be out of sight for as far north as the roads will take you: Cape Wrath or John o'Groats. The change to dour stone-built houses and clean air is like a cold shower: but the break is being eroded and smoothed down into sameness. Each year a little more goes – this is 1955's contribution, 5, north of Bolton-le-Sands. And here the fault is not the builder's: what is wrong is that he has apparently been allowed to 'choose *his* own site' as he invites the purchasers to choose theirs, when there were gaps to be filled in existing estates.

5

At Carnforth there is a view of half a hill quarried away, 6 (see opposite). 'Terrible', one could say, taking this issue in the wrong way, as a preserve-it-at-all-costs manifesto. But is it terrible? The scar is clean and sharp – it accentuates the wildness of the rest of the hill; what is wrong is the litter of dreary wartime

huts in the foreground, flabby and set down without any adaptation to the site, they deflate the whole view into an echo of the Lancashire we have left behind.

Just one lamp-post in Kendal market place, 7, but it is so overpowering, and blunders across the established dimensions so clumsily that it is impossible to look at the market place itself. Why was it put there? – there is no main road or traffic block to light; it is just callousness and the necessity to be uniform. There is no point in getting life to work smoothly if you find when you have finished that there is nothing to work for, and there is no point in making towns well lit, easy to park in and skelter through, if there is nothing left of the towns when you have finished.

KENDAL – LAKELAND

Here is Lakeland as a slight deviation from the route to show what might have been expected from the definition: that Subtopia doesn't change its forms, however beautiful the scenery. This is confirmed at Bowness, 1 and 2, with a ferocious display of Municipal gardening beside Lake Windermere. Lakesides, especially Lakeland lakesides, need a very light touch, not a barrel-organ-roll of symmetrical plots. The proper place for this horticultural display is inside a public park, which the visitor can see if he wants to, and doesn't have to

3, 4

endure, willy nilly, on his journey. Greenery in the town must always be a foil, not a focus, and in particular modern towns through their shortcomings may compel it because of the need for relief – relief from size, relief from squalor and ugly surroundings, and relief from traffic and crowds. Bowness is little more than a village, the surroundings speak for themselves, and – what is wrong with every piece of Municipal Rustic – all the flurry of traffic and crowds is reflected and intensified in the gardens, in small-scale elements and fussy detailing. The idea that they should be under the control of an UDC is a typically wrong-headed approach to Lakeland – it is a National Park, not an opportunity for municipal display.

Lakeland develops with a fine view up Langdale ruined by the squalid huts which expediency has found easier to leave than to move, 3 and 4 (see opposite). A similar effect of complete deflation is given by the petrol pumps just south of Ambleside, 5, and again at Grasmere, 6. Since the photograph was taken the Ambleside pumps have been set in their frame of reference by cleanly designed modern buildings, i.e.,

5

6

7   8   9

the blurred-edge part of Subtopia has been removed, but considering the site and the size of Lakeland, camouflage would have been better. Overcrowding has reached a point where it is impossible for all the features in our landscape to 'be themselves', however well they do it; a very sad thing. The notice at Ambleside, 7, underlines with its 'Lakes UDC', one of the points of this issue, the outward sign of the idea behind the Bowness gardens: that really the Lakes are an extension of Manchester and Newcastle projected there on asphalt fingers and in forty-foot metal containers, 8, at Ambleside and, 9, at Keswick. The charabancs are inevitable, but the country must not be charapoxed to take them. If the outskirts of Manchester and Newcastle hadn't been made so dreary, there would be less incentive to cram motor traffic into an area which can't absorb it and which is already full of walkers and mountain climbers (for whom, considering its small area and diversity, Lakeland is most suited).

Going up the Lakes 'arterial road' – Ambleside to Keswick – there is an unpleasant surprise at Thirlmere. The forestry planting at Cannock Chase was more of a social crime (in denying open spaces to an overpopulated area) than a visual one, but this attempt to turn Helvellyn into a foothill of the Carpathians, 10, is visual sadism at its worst. The Lake itself is owned by Manchester Corporation, and sports fencing and the favourite sign of Authority, 11. There are two things wrong: if it is essential that access to the reservoirs be forbidden then Lakeland is no place for reservoirs. And – so small, yet so symptomatic – there is a moral obligation on 'M.C.W.W.' to explain courteously and not prohibit with a verbal slap in the face.

10   11

MULTIPLE USE

Here are three sterilized landscapes – open country at New Oscott destroyed between the wars by Birmingham sprawl, 1; limbo at Blackburn, a mixture of derelict ground, housing and industry, 2; and the side of Helvellyn prevented from being either landscape or climbing ground, 3. Subtopia on three different sites produced in three different ways. There is a way of reducing this to the misuse of one site, not three: superimpose them, put planting *and* dense housing into the limbo, releasing Green Belt for Birmingham, and a vital part of the Lake District for the whole country.

That is only the negative side. The drawing, 4 (see opposite), shows the sort of landscape that could result from imaginative treatment of multiple use, for it is a means to better towns in its own right as well as being one way of attacking Subtopia. Industry and housing, commercial traffic and pedestrian square, cranes and trees, pub and warehouse, all superimposed, not segregated into zoned areas – 'residential', 'industrial', 'recreational', and so on. When put together they interact to give virility, not chaos: and when segregated they are amputated sections looking for a town to take part in – as can be seen in some of the New Towns, where zoning has been carried through thoroughly from the start. The sum of so many planned watertight areas is an area and not a place; its character is still that of the separate areas plus the concrete road-and-lamppost sticking-plaster that binds them together. And as all towns get the zoning treatment they will all come to look alike in the components and they will all cease to have any character as a whole – which is Subtopia redefined.

LAKELAND – CARLISLE

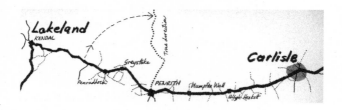

At the top of the Honister Pass, beyond Keswick, there is an extraordinary collection, 1 and 2, which is the quintessence of present-day Lakeland: a quarry doing a good job, but an eyesore nevertheless with its squalid huts, which won't come beautiful on their own; a youth hostel in cosy weatherboard for the walkers and, an AA hut for the use of vehicles which can't get up, or down, the 1-in-4 slopes each way. The result is disillusion, and the remedy – don't build where you will tame wildness,

unless you have to: and if you do, build hard, not soft. Of the three the quarry is most of an eyesore, but it is built 'hard' and gives least offence to the site. The hostel is just like a dorm, at a farm camp, and the AA Hut standardised Subtopia. None would be worth making a fuss about *if England were big enough to lose them.*

Beyond Penrith, there are derelict huts at Plumpton Wall, 3 (see opposite), with a prohibition still stuck to the broken half-gate, 4 (see opposite). Certainly the decaying huts and rusting installations are no incentive to a closer look. But what sort of an idea of visual responsibility has the body which, ten years after the war, has done nothing about its eyesores but plaster them with curt notices?

The County Council has caught the disease, 5, and what seems at first sight to be justifiable indignation in a good cause (there is nothing like an English tourist for enjoying the country and then leaving so much litter that nobody else can do so) is seen as another command from Authority. Although there is good reason

5 6

for it, when attached to an inelegant tub of wire and concrete it becomes more of a nuisance than the litter it was put there to prevent, since the litter would only be litter but the litter box, because of its overtones of public parks and the way in which it robs the land-scape of spontaneity, destroys a whole atmosphere. In a well-known beauty-parking place or at a resort the proportion might well be reversed. It is the genius loci again, and the whole problem of Subtopia would never have existed if those who developed, improved, or only preserved places (the preservationists are as sinister as the exploiters) thought in terms of character as well as convenience.

Now the familiar outrages begin to make fare-well appearances. England came in with a skein of wire at Southampton: here it goes out with one at

Carlisle, 6 (see previous page). Roundabouts were beautified in Hampshire; here they are in Cumberland, 7; and if the cen-tre of Oxford was full of cars, the centre of Carlisle has every-thing else, 8–10 (see opposite). It is as if all the hirelings of the road in this battle of Town v. Road has massed for one last attack – traffic, bus shelters, lamp standards and beacons, with a fifth column of public lavatories, 10. Who can walk in the centre of Carlisle and not feel that man has become a pawn in his own game?

7

8   9   10

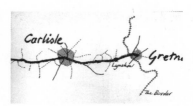

On this route to the Border, a bit of beautifying at Stanwix, 1, anticipates the horrible results that Scotsmen can devise when allowed to rhapsodise on the bonny and quaint, and Scotland itself greets the traveller at Gretna, 2-4. Take your choice, prefab. estate to an Ordnance factory, 2, or Auld Smiddy Road House, 3; callous eyesore or genteel blurring-of-edges. That could stand as a summing up of England – your England.

The gap: Between Gretna and the Highlands there is a hundred miles of Lowland Scotland. It has been omitted in order to make the shock of meeting a relatively unspoilt wild landscape more complete, and not because it is free from Subtopia – the twenty miles stretch from Glasgow to Loch Lomond would fill a book in itself.

THE HIGHLANDS

Opposite, above, heights of Trotternish, Skye, and below, the view south from the summit of Bidean nam Bian, Argyll.

The large circles indicate afforestation, and are proportional to the
extent of planting, but do not show actual boundaries.
The small circles are power stations.
The lines are trunk roads.

– The Highlands –

On the map opposite is the only big area of Great Britain that is still wild. It is also the only big area in Great Britain with undeveloped agricultural and industrial resources. It is a part of Scotland that Lowland Scots feel they have a moral duty to develop and improve after the early nineteenth-century clearances and 150 years of neglect: it is also an area whose inhabitants, by and large, would welcome the improvement but not the development.

Which is the right course, in the light of the human and industrial refuse tip that England – and South Scotland – is becoming? The *Review* is emphatically on the side of the Highlander – improve but don't develop. The best use of the Highlands in an industrialised Britain is to provide a lung remote from industrial development and big enough to lose oneself in. A lung that is deliberately hard to get at and must be explored on foot, to provide a change of life and not merely a change of scene. In Norway, such an area – hundreds of square miles of it – is actually included, protected from development, inside the Oslo city boundaries; Glasgow could do the same if it wanted to. Even from the point of view of economics that is in the end far more important to a balanced Great Britain than a bit more electric power or a few more aluminium pots and pans. In return it is a cheap price to make life for the Highlander as comfortable – as cushioned even – as it can possibly be. Hydro in the Highlands for the Highlands, yes; to swell the National Grid, no.

That, however, is just theorising, to make it quite clear what the *Review*'s basic attitude is. In practice, as the map shows, there are already dozens of forestry sites, dozens of power stations. For these, WHAT and WHERE are decided for us, and the question is the visual one – the fundamental visual question – of HOW. Existing sites can tell us things about WHAT and WHERE (sadly, more often about WHAT NOT and WHERE NOT), and although the *Review* is not setting up as a land planner, when it sees what it thinks is self-evident landscape wrecking it must say so.

And when we look at HOW, an odd thing happens. There is the pons asinorum of design, that of reconciling modern architecture and tradition, that comes out clearly enough in a sequence of housing or power stations; but far more important, in the total effect, is the trim. In England there are so many conflicting elements in any landscape, so many sets of trims or anti-trims, that one can rarely surprise a straightforward problem that is free from half a dozen other interlocking problems. In the Highlands, with abundant air and moorland surroundings, each fault in detailing becomes startlingly clear.

So macrocosm comes back to microcosm and not only in the abstract (from the hydro scheme to the handrail on the bridge) but in a personal way as well. For, per head, the Highlands has more litter left around with less care than anywhere else in the country. It is the social failure of the tourists: it surely must also be (as at Lochcarron on pages 148–9) the couldn't-care-lessness of the natives. It doesn't matter which, except that the fact that both are to blame prevents the litter being pinned one side or the other of an inter-island squabble. What is important is that at last there is personal responsibility for some part of Subtopia, and at last the elements of the problem have thinned out so that the essentials are clear. In the 'shredded gumboots of the proud Gael', or the sauce carton on the heather, we have reached the well-spring of the urge to dump, indifferent to visual effect. Subtopia is the legalisation of the urge to dump on a national scale.

Most people, publicly anyway, would express abhorrence of leaving litter (whatever they do privately in Inverness-shire when the dustman forgets to call, or in a more permanent way, in mid-Surrey when they build their home). The dislike of litter and the recognition of individual responsibility are common ground, and it only needs extension, not change, for this dislike of litter to become a public litter-conscience, reacting to litter in its widest sense, whoever or whatever dumps it (and august names some of the worst dumpers have, too). It is a basis for creating a climate of dissent that will turn out to be of the same family as the radical principle elucidated in Townscape, *A.R.*, December, 1949.

Man and cultivated land in harmony with the wild: Skerray, North Sutherland. Notice that this is unequivocally twentieth century man – the car and lorry, the corrugated iron roofs, the cemented jetty. But it is a supreme example of instinctive feeling for landscape in the way the elements are used – the HOW – an innate tact that makes even the neatest piece of present day town planning look at the same time overdesigned and boorish.

First, a reminder that we have not finished with the components of Subtopia that are already so familiar because we have moved to the Highlands. They are just less dense, that's all. Here is a selection:

... multiple wire at Fort William

... fragmented market place at Beauly

... anti-urbanism at Inverness

... derelict camps at Evanton

... Things in Fields at Tyndrum

... wire in villages at Carrbridge

Housing

The simplest interaction of man and the wild is when he builds dwellings on it. A short list of what can go wrong – the Roads to Ruin – may indicate the thought process likely to take place when any item has to be fitted into the landscape.

To start with, there is the harmony that everyone would like to reproduce, at Skerray, 1. This contains in itself a greater step than any which perplex us: from primitive to civilised – black hut to Victorian shieling. Both are part of the landscape – one instinctively, almost in an animal way, the other consciously, but not self-consciously – i.e., it is the landscape that is being expressed, not the ego.

With that example, how many ways can the design go wrong? There are in fact four main Roads to Ruin.

A. It can turn its back on visual problems altogether – back to the blind approach of the black hut without the instinctive fitness and feeling for materials that redeemed it. In other words a dump, and all the more of a shock for being on the West Coast of Scotland, 2.

B. It can go genteel: and how little it need go is emphasised by adjoining true-and-false cottages at Shieldaig, 3. Just a matter of a few degrees of roof pitch, two fatal mullions in the dormers, six panes instead of one to the front door, little reminiscences of Outer Dundee: shieling into council house. Or it can take the inevitable next step and become the national suburban style fully grown: so far, only scattered, but insidiously spreading – Mair, Ross & Cromarty, 4, and Kinlochleven, 5.

C. It can remember that the houses need visual attention and forget that the trim needs just as much, as at Stornoway, 6. If both houses and trim are unattended, the result is just one more standard housing estate, like Kinlochleven, 7, all the worse for its impressive backcloth.

D. It can litter the land – 8, Stirling: flat roofs, striking layouts and prairie planning. You might as well be looking south from Mill Hill: genius loci, regional character and landscape patterns are all ignored.

8

E. What happens if it goes modern, not modernistic? There are few enough examples – these Forestry Commission chalets near Tomdoun on Loch Garry come nearest to it, 9. They are not ideal, but they do have the same fundamental characteristic as the houses at Skerray, 1 – they are *in* the landscape, not on it.

9

Roads

Here we have the clearest application of the advice: improve but don't develop. The old Highland roads were a hair-raising experience – some of them still are. They brought mountaineering within the reach of every robust car, but for the Highlander they made a difficult life intolerable. 'Improvement', as economy dictates anyway, means resisting the temptation to make autobahnen: metal instead the single-track roads and provide passing places. They can cope with local traffic, they daunt the tepid majority and to those who are prepared to meet the country half way they repay a bonus in Highland courtesy that transforms a day's drive: and from having to stop at passing places it is an easy step to getting out and walking from them.

'Development' means trying to imitate the trunk network of the rest of the country. How little is needed to change a road from component to dominant is shown in 1 and 2: above, an unimproved road (Loch Tay – Glen Lyon), and below, a road that has just gone over the edge into dreariness (B.939, Tomintoul – Cock Bridge) by the thinnest of margins; just a straight road-line that got standardised fences parcelling it off from the landscape instead of the careful trim treatment it needed.

From there it is an easy stage to 3, beginning to look like something from an estate layout, and 4, part of A82 north of Fort William. The final stages – badly sited multiple carriageways and their beautification – have not affected the Highlands – yet: and to show what can be done, here is a new road to Benevan Dam, 5, that far from destroying the appearance of wildness, enhances it by curling elegantly and free of knick-knacks (wire, fences, curbs) round the shelf between loch and rocks.

Tourism

The adaptation of the idea of improvement but not development from roads to their users is quite clear. The Highlands are the only area left in Britain where one can return to wild nature without the Scylla and Charybdis of a municipal rubbish tip and a rustique sign saying 'footpath to Heather Dingle.' That is a far more important service than providing one more scenic drive, breathtaking though the scenery is. Nor must expansion of tourism degenerate into mass tourism: a hundred charas a day from Scourie to Lochinver, and a hundred garages and motels to serve them. If you want to come on the landscape's terms you are welcome: but if you want another mass holiday-behind-perspex with all mod. cons. you must find it elsewhere.

Of the inevitable effect on the landscape of indiscriminate opening out, here is one small but significant symptom, 1, the asphalted path made down to the falls of Measach, near Ullapool, so that the tourists from the buses which stop at the top shan't get their feet muddy. The result is to convert a frightening 600 foot deep gash into an echo of one of the chines at Bournemouth – specialised but very vicious Subtopia.

1

Here are more aspects of the two sides: intelligent expansion, represented by the inconspicuous resting place, 2 (Inverkirkaig, Sutherland), the small steamer, 3 (Loch Katrine), and the leisurely motorist, 4 (Loch Maree) and mass mechanised tourism in the rows of buses, 5 (Portree), the genteel cott and the genteel flower garden which serve them, 6 and 7 (both near Fort William).

Afforestation

Again largely a matter of HOW, though remarks on WHERE cannot be repressed, wrung out by the sight of landscape massacre. There are numbers of spoiled South-Highland glens that would benefit from afforestation – but not the austere and once noble Glen Shiel on the road to Skye. There are miles of sodden moorland along the main roads that have lost their remoteness and never had grandeur, to which conifers would come as a welcome relief – for example almost all of A.9 from Blair Atholl to Inverness, 2, with its accompaniment of railway-and-wire plus telegraph poles-arid-wire plus pylons-and-wire – but not to blur the magical landscapes of the far north-west. Finally, there are dozens of scenes like this one in Skye – overgrown clachans – that need intelligent tying-up with small-scale planting, 1.

1

2

And as for HOW, what is already there shows all the English mistakes seen in even sharper relief because of the settings: blanket forestry, 3 (see overleaf), at Drumtochty – just no thought that the land surface might have any other significance but to give a quick yield. Repudiation of contours, 4, beside Loch Long (see overleaf); the only contour that has been acknowledged is the line above which trees won't grow economically. If you don't think that there could ever be forestry as brutal as Thirlmere (on page 116), look at this in Glen Shiel, 5 (see overleaf): it is almost a mirror image. Coming back to the trim, which always contains the faults in a nutshell, look at this fence – also in Glen Shiel, 6. What an awful piece of muddled thinking, or bone headed indifference; any garage mechanic would soon tell you what he thought of it as a job neatly done.

Hydro-electricity

If hydro-electricity and the Highlands are to come together, one or the other must capitulate: the issue is as bald as that. In the circumstances, it must obviously be hydro-electricity that capitulates, for there is too much at stake. This does not mean proscribing it altogether – though the *Review* thinks it bad long-term economics to endanger our only remaining big open space for a little extra power – but it does mean extreme care in siting and detailing so that the effect of exploitation is reduced to a minimum. This can be done in two ways, well-designed buildings and well-camouflaged buildings. Well-designed, unhappily, is not enough by itself. It would be if the country was as big as Siberia, but it can't be said too often that this isn't just another bit of wild country, it is the last available bit of wild country. Camouflage means siting the buildings in the least conspicuous places, with inconspicuous entrances and exits, and planting for concealment. The ramshackle appearance of 1 is all the more pointed by comparison with the assimilated Scots Baronial house in the background, and the neo-Classical trim of 2 (see overleaf) all the more inappropriate for being patently a junction-box for wires and pipes.

The pipes themselves should go underground, or appear to go underground, and ditto for wires and pylons, 3–6 (see overleaf). In their present form they act like concrete lampstandards, and by association reduce to sameness with the Subtopian scene the one landscape that still has a personality of its own. Even when they are handsome in themselves, as pylons often are, elements that are standard to many landscapes reduce visibility, so to speak, to nil. Variety vanishes; only the samenesses remain.

Trim

The architectural standard of most of the hydro-electric power
stations is not high: however, some of the detailing is good – for
instance, the dam on Loch Tummel, 1. The contrasting photographs
point the moral. There is detail which looks frighteningly Fascist, 6
(see overleaf), at Loch Sloy, or pompously Classic, 7 (see overleaf),
but there is also a cadre of light handrails, 2, and unaffected concrete
construction, 3. There are dowdy seats and steps, 8 (see overleaf):
there are also crisp seats, 4, and simple clean-limbed steps and rails,
5. There are standard Midland-gasworks entrances, 10 (see overleaf),
and Midland lamp standards, 9 (see overleaf) . . . and that is the
crux. The landscape in 9 could be in the Midlands; the mountain
background has become devalued, one ceases to take it into account.
This, in fact, is Subtopia, expressed in terms of one ugly concrete

pole and a great big pipe. Why? – and why does it happen only to the bad examples – why isn't the scene blurred with thought of Waterloo Bridge in 2 and any English canal in 5? There are two reasons for the superiority of 1–5: first because the trim is content to be a component, and second because the solution looks functionally right, and fitness carries its own passport wherever it turns up. The difference is between the standardisation that makes all places look alike and the standardisation that looks right for all places: the difference between Subtopia and the Functional Tradition.

The alternative of good trim is bad trim, and this in its crudest form is what jars most in a Highland tour. The land surface is just used as dump (see opposite)– for aluminium plant, 1, quarries, 2, disused cars, 3, sheds and oil drums, 4, re-used buses, 5, right down to one single (and in its context, at the top of Glencoe, one sickening)

146

watering can, 6. The first example was put up by a national company: the last was thrown down by some single 'person unknown.' Because of the background, and the lack of those traditional English tips, ditches and copses, the offences are much more obvious, and it becomes possible to sort out individual contributions. Here, as a quintessence, is an even more personal example, 7 and 8 (see overleaf) . . .

. . . so the whole problem of Subtopia in all the square miles of Great Britain comes down to this: one traveller's private defecation on the old military road south of Inverness. Here at last is visual couldn't-care-less-ness isolated, a matter of individual responsibility, after all the pages of boards and offices and departments. It is almost a relief: it is also the starting point for the slow climb back to sanity. The first steps are obvious, the elementary visual hygiene needed to make us house-trained in our outdoor room. But after that, when it comes to judging the way in which our surroundings are changed for us? We may have no opportunity to plan them directly, but we can at least create an atmosphere of intelligent dissent to Subtopia; and some of the means are indicated on pp. 151–160.

7   8

Microcosm

Finally, part of a journey which seems to have been deliberately designed as a Morality play for the Highlands – the view across Loch Carron, Ross and Cromarty, seen on the way south from Achnasheen to Strome Ferry (see opposite). In each case the background stays the same (indicated by the arrowed island) – and across the foreground parade the standard elements of Subtopia: first the view uncompromised, 1, then obsolete petrol pumps as a jarring component, 2, and as the obscuring dominant, 3. Then an individual mess, 4, and idiotic planting, 5: and finally the foreground treated as it should be treated by its owner (each plot is the frontage to a house across the road) – treated that is as a base for the view instead of a way of fouling it. If you have the special luck to live on the waterfront of Loch Carron why not in mere self-interest enjoy it?

– Summing Up –

T his section is intended for the man-in-the-street, rather than for architects and planners, to whom the points it makes may seem over-simplified, or over-obvious. One reason for Subtopia is that nobody has bothered to indicate its effects in terms that the man-in-the-street can see as relevant, and the recommendations below are therefore phrased in terms an architect would use if he were trying to sum up the argument to a layman.

Manifesto

Places are different: Subtopia is the annihilation of the difference by attempting to make one type of scenery standard for town, suburb, countryside and wild.

So what has to be done is to maintain and intensify the difference between places. This is the basic principle of visual planning.

It is also the end to which all the other branches of planning – sociology, traffic circulation, industry, housing hygiene – are means.

They all attempt to make life more rewarding, more healthy, less pointlessly arduous. But if they at

the same time destroy our environment they are denying us the end to which they were designed to be the
means. We get the by-products, lose the end-product.

This happens because everyone is a specialist
whose aim is not primarily to achieve the end-product.
The planning department which tries to co-ordinate
them is using rules which apply nominally to the end-
product but these, because they have been divorced
from the visual imagination which conceived them,
have become ciphers.

What is lacking is someone who stands outside
all the specialisation and does the visual thinking,
someone with sufficient powers to carry out his visual
integration: responsible nationally, not locally, and
responsible for topographical entities, not administrative ones.

That is the inside job, a hope for the future.

But the future will be too late. The action is
needed *NOW*.

So the attack must come from outside. That is a
job for all of us, and the only qualification we need is
to have eyes to see.

You *have* eyes to see if you have been exasperated
by the lunacies exposed in these pages; if you think
they represent a universal levelling down and grey-
ing out; if you think that they should be fought, not
accepted.

Your armoury is your ability to see and reason;
your target is the stuff shown here.

To help your aim, below is a list of *precepts*, tempering counsels to interpose between indignation and action.

And to make the target clearer, a *checklist of malpractices* for you to correlate in your own home area.

Don't be afraid that you will be just one individual registering dissent. It is *your* country that is being defaced, it belongs to *you*, and as an individual amongst fifty million individuals, not a 'set of income groups' or an 'electorate'.

So use your double birthright – as a free-thinking human being and as a Briton lucky enough to be born into a country where the individual voice can still get a hearing.

Planning decisions and changes in the land surface surround you every day. In each of them a site may be imploring your aid.

The first thing is to be able to see and feel. If you have come with us this far, you can; that is the premise we make in our call to arms.

Then to know your local area inside out, whether it is a Surrey suburb, the middle of Swansea or the Yorkshire Wolds.

Then to reach your decision on a change or projected change. Your *own* decision, not ours; not blurred by sentiment or social pressure or economic pressure. A matter that is purely between you and the site, without any pressure.

Then to act, and to know how to act; whether singly or in concert, to the newspapers or the Ministry; to know what outrage the planning authority can stop and what outrage it is submitting to from lack of support; to know when preservationists will help and when they will be unable to see your point; to know which points from your argument should be put to the borough engineer, and which to the chairman of the council.

Each success makes the next one easier; each failure may by its repercussions prevent a repetition.

But act, if only to write a letter. In trying to keep intact the identity of your environment you will maintain your own as well.

Precepts

1 This is 1955. You can't put the clock back. More than that, today's complexity is to be welcomed, not endured. It is not the technology that is wrong, but the false applications of it.

2 Three things have got to be accepted about Britain – it is industrial, overcrowded and small. These all suggest one conclusion, that all our development must be high-density and small-area. High-density industrial belts, with buffers of true country in between. High-density towns, with their population neither spreading outwards nor decanted evenly, but put back into the centre. Consequently, there

will be high-density countryside, i.e., really rural or wild, not eroded by splinter towns or industry. And this conclusion, which is sociological common sense, is part of the visual solution too. If towns are towns and country is country, they have gone a long way towards being allowed to be themselves.

3 The alternative is blurred edges. Blurred edges may come from standardisation. It is not the standardisation which is wrong – look at canals – but how it is standardised. Standard fittings are like the nuts and bolts of a Meccano set: the model is put together with them, but they don't dominate the finished product because they are unobtrusive, subordinate and impersonal.

4 Forget preconceptions. The site's the thing, not a set of rules, and your eye's the thing, not the textbook. Look first, then decide, and only then find a rule to fit your decision.

Checklist of malpractices

Town

—does traffic which has nothing to do with your town steamroller through it?

—has the town surrendered to it, by driving a boulevard through, or inserting a roundabout in, the old centre. Does the traffic as a result get heavier and faster, and the pedestrian life of the town more and more islanded?

—or has the town lost its centre to the car park? or the open square to a wired-in public garden?

—what is the municipal solution to a gap in the main street: rebuilding, or conversion into a small garden or 'temporary' car park?

—how many of your town's traffic roundabouts have rustic planting? Why?

—is your town in decay? Is the area behind its main streets a waste of cleared old housing, made into car parks or kept as vacant lots; and are there at the same time sprawling estates on the outskirts?

—could you walk to work if there was a transport strike? Can you walk to the country in an evening, if you want to? Or are you unable to do *either*?

—how about historic buildings? Are they allowed to look old, or are they given a 'quaint' face-lift under the excuse of preservation?

—and are the best eighteenth-century buildings preserved? or only those which reflect a travel-poster Merrie England of beams and tracery.

—are the natural trees respected, or ruthlessly lopped when there is no need for it? Or are they grubbed up altogether, and ornamental trees and flowering shrubs planted instead? The suburb, not the town, is the place for ornamental trees.

—do wires take a back seat in the view or a front one?

Suburb

—is it still *rus-in-urbe*? Has the traffic engineer respected the scale, or driven across it and made a mockery of the illusion?

—has it ever been *rus-in-urbe*? Are you living in a true suburb or just a bit of spec. builders' quick profit-making?

—is the country farther away than it was in 1939? How far? At that rate when will it disappear and your suburb run into the next one?

—does your local planning office obey the letter or the spirit of amenity control? Has it allowed further encroachment on the countryside, on the grounds that it is next to 'existing development'. And has it rejected designs for modern houses because they wouldn't be in conformity with 'existing development'.

—can you take a country walk?

—can your wife pop down to the shops or is it a fag without a car?

—can you walk round to the local or do you drive there?

—do the pram-pushers have a bad time when it's raining; do the streets seem too long and too wide?

—this is the home of ornamental trees and shrubs. Are there so many that it seems like fairyland? There ought to be.

—are they urbanising the scene with giant lighting standards?

Country

—how many Things in Fields are there in your parish?

—are they indispensable? Have you any idea why they are there at all? Has any attempt been made to camouflage them?

—have you an airfield or military camp? Is it disused, or has it disused sub-sites, and, if so, are they likely to be cleared up?

—is your village affected by urban sprawl—are there speculative estates built to serve the nearest town?

—if there is an arterial road, has it brought a trail of cafés and garages strung out from one parish boundary to the other?

—and has it got careless siting and inappropriate planting to try to cover it up, or was it landscaped from the start?

—how about afforestation? Have you a conifer forest, was it the right type of site for conifers, and has the planting been done well? Or is it the familiar pattern of blanket and swath? Did it eat up open ground you used to walk on? Can you even get into it now?

—how many types of wire are there in the parish? Standing on the green, how many wires can you see clearly? Could any be put underground, or sited less obtrusively?

—how many cottages have fallen down in the last ten years? How many are decaying now? Has the council tried to convert them? And is it building new houses on the site, or away on the edge of the village?

—if it *is* building new houses on the outskirts is there any difference between them and the estate in the next village, or the suburbs of your nearest town? Why isn't there, when the villages and the town are markedly different?

—what does your visual profit-and-loss schedule since 1939 look like?

Wild

—how wild is it, how far from a town? Is the official policy to preserve it entirely, or have a nibble of industry here and a nibble of housing there?

—does the W.D. own any of it? What for, and must it be done here? Has it brought a trail of camps and roads and made it a little Aldershot? Should it have been evacuated after the war, but has been kept instead by a breach of faith?

—when you stand and listen how many unnatural sounds do you hear? A train? a car? a plane? distant target practice? a rifle range? the odd bomb?

—is the open heath or down being rapidly enclosed by wire fences?

—are there notice boards and red flags to warn you off?

—are the rights of way kept open?

—do you ever feel civilisation is a long way off?

—is it being 'opened up' for the tourists or are they coming on the landscape's own terms? Is everything made easy for the tepid majority – motels, cafés, motorways – or are the facilities kept simple for those prepared to walk their way around?

– Anthology –

To conclude, there is a short anthology of the philosophical background to Subtopia stated in its widest terms, from the nineteenth-century prophecy to its fulfilment today, and the extension – mankind's reaction to its self-made mess.

'It is the main factory of the Elmdown Aircraft Company Limited, which is known to be doing quite a good job. It is tucked away into a misty hollow in the South Midlands, with a long flat space behind for the airfield. It's all okay. Rather out of the way, of course, ten miles from the nearest town, but that was what was wanted . . . One of our grandfathers, suddenly arriving here, would have thought somebody had gone mad. From the old-fashioned standpoint, there's a kind of lunacy about the place. The very road outside the factory does not seem to belong to that country at all, and might have been hastily unrolled there like a vast gritty carpet. The factory itself, when it stops being a toy village with painted trees and meadows, looks as if it had not been built there but brought from some distant city and dropped by the roadside, as if a giant child, using the whole country as its sand-pit, had picked the thing up and then idly poked it into position with an immense forefinger. Half a dozen liners, jammed together between those low green hills, would hardly look more out of place.'

J. B. Priestley: *Daylight on Saturday*, Reprint Society.

1. THE THEME

'The culture of a nation by general consent would, I suppose, be regarded as its greatest heritage, but a heritage perhaps equally worthy of being cherished is the land surface which a nation occupies. The culture to a large extent must have been influenced by the character of the land surface, and in any event culture and land surface are interwoven, and interreact in countless directions difficult to unravel. For better or for worse a nation may endeavour to mould and to develop its culture along definite and preconceived lines. In whatsoever direction the national character and the nation's activities move, the land surface and the use to which it has been, and is being, put will be the mirror which reflects the devious paths which a people have trodden in search of self expression.'

Sir George Stapledon: *The Land Now and Tomorrow*, Faber and Faber.

2. THE PARABLE

'October 16th. Towards the end of the day, a grey bird circled round us for a long time trying to settle. At nightfall, in obvious distress, it perched on the rudder head – a singularly uncomfortable position. I picked it up and put it down on the deck, out of the wind, between the shorelegs and the pram. Farge offered it some biscuit, some fresh water and even a little fish that had been washed into the scuppers. But the bird would accept nothing. It merely wanted to go to sleep, which it did, very peacefully . . . With the dawn, the bird was still on the deck, and apparently feeling better, for it swallowed the fish Farge tendered it once more in one gulp. During the morning, it rose and flew away, having fouled the deck in no uncertain manner. Its ingratitude seemed almost human.'

Le Toumelin: *Kurun*, Rupert Hart-Davis.

3. THE PREDICTION

'The world is about to come to an end . . . Typical victims of the inexorable moral laws, we shall perish by the thing by which we thought to live. Machinery will have so much Americanised us, progress will have so much atrophied our spiritual element, that nothing in the sanguinary, blasphemous of unnatural dreams of the Utopians can be compared to what will actually happen . . . Those times are perhaps quite close at hand. Who knows whether they are not here already; whether it is not simply the coarsening of our nature that prevents us from perceiving the atmosphere that we already breathe?'

Charles Baudelaire: *Fusées*, 1862. trans. Weidenfeld and Nicholson.

4. THE FULFILMENT

'The horror can be very big. But it can also be very small . . . it is, mark you, a thing of opposite extremes. Litter – litter for its own sake – plays a large part in it; but so also does a certain terrifying kind of soulless cleanliness I think inanity, futility, and a certain ghastly "gim-crackism" are elements in it too . . . What are called the "Residential Sections" of the big cities reek and stink of this terrifying Presence. But you can find it too, as I have hinted, on any amusement beach, or in any amusement park. It has a wraith-like quality, it has a death-like quality, it has about it some queer ultimate desolation of emptiness, but with all this, and here lies the paradox of its shuddering horribleness, it is brand-new, spick-and-span, and strident . . . Take all this and add to it the most vividly realised spiritual desolation of T. S. Eliot's Wasteland and then add to that the tough, callous and brutal veneer, shiny surfaces over stale perspiration, of a rich "Summer Resort" and you will get some idea of the atmosphere I am trying to indicate, wherein all that is standardised and dispiriting groans with a rocker, flaps with an awning, sways with rusty-dusty evergreens, and gapes with a million empty garages.'

John Cowper Powys: *Autobiography*, John Lane, The Bodley Head.

* * *

'Between Abingdon and Wantage, the first four thousand, the second fifteen hundred years old, I passed the village of Drayton. All that remained of Drayton's ego was a secretive grouping of buildings down a side-street, a fine isolated barn standing alone in the middle of a field and a pair of cottages about two hundred yards away. Their incongruity with Drayton's new being was grotesque. On the left of the road stood a row of gigantic elm-tree butts and behind these a line of bunga-lunguses, on whose behalf the ancient elms had been beheaded. Between the butts and the rash of makeshift buildings, the ground was scarified of every blade of grass; it was nothing but a scab. The houses had no view, no structural motive, no positional relation to anything about them. They just stood there in a kind of horrible vacancy and stared at the corpses of the trees they had destroyed. Some would have called the act pitiable, others philistine, others downright wicked. The thought that came to me was its rank stupidity.'

H. J. Massingham: *Through the Wilderness*, Cobden-Sanderson.

* * *

'The things I saw did not compass the hundredth part of a devastation flung far and wide over England. Even the little towns help to spread it. They throw out their feelers just as the big towns throw out their suburbs.

First, the arterial road; next the houses along its rims clinging like green fly to a stem; then tributary roads boring into the adjacent country with their "desirable frontages."'

Ibid.

* * *

'The phrase commonly used to describe the process I had witnessed over a small area of the square mileage it covers in all parts of the country is the "cult of ugliness." It is an unwise expression because nobody cultivates ugliness which comes, frequently enough, of the cult of prettiness. One of the terrors of our times is that ugliness comes unsought, unconscious and unsuspected. A more correct definition, I think, would be the cult of sameness, nor is it an exaggeration to term that cult a scourge of pestilence that, like the locust, devours the country naked. That is what a country so built over becomes, naked, because that which clothed it in a presence of its own, which gave it individual form and so reality, has been stripped away from it. Henceforward, it is neuter; it has no selfhood.'

Ibid.

* * *

'It might be said that the country of my journey was naturally dull. But the dullest country possesses its own rights and seal of particularity to distinguish it from other regions. But this particularity, which I might call the soul of place . . . had been smoothed out as some projection in the road is crunched level by the steam-roller. The country I traversed might have been any-where: it was adrift from landmarks, set in the void, an expressionless mask. It was not the garages and petrol stations, the villas and bungalows, the road arteries, all those winged words of the machine, which appalled me. It was, I repeat, the disappearance of identity, and it reminded me of that form of sleepy sickness which strikes all animation, every difference, all emotion and light out of the human face and leaves it only a plaster cast. I got lost four times in this country, but I was trav-elling on and on without getting anywhere, without passing anything or leaving anything behind.'

Ibid.

* * *

'How indeed should the traveller recognise the differ-ence between one town or village and another along a complex system of roads, when new houses throw an almost continuous chain between them, and all of them stamped with the neutralizing anonymity and uniformity of mass-production? Fragments only were left of the marks of distinction both in position and character which used to separate one place from another, Twyford from Wokingham and Wokingham from Bracknell. Their unique identities had been filched away from them and they had become practically as alike as a row of peas in a pod. But even peas in a pod are independent of an umbilical cord attaching each to each and one to all. These towns, deprived of that separateness which gave unto each its name, were chained together like one of the old convict gangs by the ribbon development of the main roads. The stringing of beads on a string had not only levelled down the identity of town and village, but had pressed out and filled in the features of the country that lay between them. This country had become nothing but a line of distance, curved or straight, long or short, from one place without a name to another.'

Ibid.

* * *

'The people who built our cathedrals and parish churches, our barns, cottages and manor-houses had far less feeling for the face of the land they made more beautiful than our latter-day migrants who deface it with the pimples in which they live. A devil has entered in upon them which we call to-day vulgarity and blindness to values of truth and beauty (though not, I think, to goodness), and the industrial system has destroyed their resistance to its passage. But the love is there, it is a reality, a love of beauty and the nature which bore them, but which they have been deprived of the power to cherish and understand. Their omnipresent gardens bear witness both to this love and their weakness in making something of it.'

    Ibid.

* * *

'The camp-followers brought up the rear of the older type of barbarian invaders. To-day, they go before the van of the country-loving host. They are the speculative builders, and their share in the paradox is to destroy the country, the craving for which has set the multitude upon the march. *E pur si muove.* Onward, Christian soldiers! That there is no country left where the migrants settle, makes no difference neither to the quest itself nor to the satisfaction which attends it goal . . . The vast majority of the new settlers are totally unaware of the fact that their notion of living in the country is an illusion. That which they sought, which moved them out into a novel environment and for whose sake they taxed their purses and broke their habits, has dissolved like the fabric of a dream. What most of them have got is a bad imitation of their urban setting, houses to the left of them, houses to the right of them, all the spit of their own, rows of shops, perhaps Woolworth's and a cinema, fenced back-yards, and a view over to the next suitable building plot. But everything is all right: they are living in the country.'

    Ibid.

5. THE MAN

'The estate where I had first built my own house was by now rapidly becoming built up and the house was almost surrounded. My wife and I had talked this over and, if we could find a spot more suitable, we decided to make a move as we had been in that house now about ten years. We went around the district at week-ends to see if we could find a less-crowded spot in the country and eventually found a suitable site at Wolvey.'

The Illustrated Carpenter and Builder, April 15, 1955: *Recollections of a Life in the Building Trade.*

6. THE MASSES

'An enormous part of the energy and ingenuity of industrial activity (I will not call it either life or civilization) goes into making it possible for more human beings to be alive at one time. This is entirely disadvantageous, and promises in time to become catastrophic. One might think that two thousand five hundred million brains would serve the cause of consciousness better than a few hundred million. But this is not true; small populations put out as many flowers of imaginative or intellectual genius as do large, and often very many more. How wonderful if it were otherwise, and the New Elizabethan Age in Britain with its fifty-five million brains could give us ten times as much poetry, drama, philosophy, song as the five million of the old Elizabethans.'

Jacquetta Hawkes: *Man on Earth*, Cresset Press.

* * *

'Great numbers are a positive evil in the morality of consciousness. The need to put roofs over their heads ruins natural beauty, and makes towns so huge as to become in large part destructive of civilised living instead of its very heart and essence. History has by now had time to prove that moderately sized, non-industrial cities, where writers, poets, painters, philosophers, statesmen, foreign visitors, and wealthy dilettanti habitually meet and mingle, dropping in on one another, meeting casually in public and in eating and drinking places, make the finest of all hotbeds for producing the prize blooms of consciousness. With modern cities, where millions live in utter social incoherence, it is quite otherwise. The longing to escape from them, coupled with the ridiculous separation of man from his work, leads to slaughter, stench, further corruption of natural beauty and a most hideous waste of a great part of the spare time which industry claims to have won for us.'

Ibid.

7. THE MASS PSYCHOLOGY

'This urge to mingle with the universe and with life as a whole and not merely with the human species is latent in every urban dweller and shows itself in many ways. It shows itself in the desire to keep pets, to associate with species other than *homo sapiens*. The number of dogs (as estimated by those that are licensed) has increased in recent years out of all proportion to the population . . . The dog, the cat, the pigeons, the window box, or the minute little garden patch all afford some measure of escape from the baneful influences of an exaggerated mass psychology – an escape from the everlasting mental contact with other human beings.'

Sir George Stapledon: *The Land Now and Tomorrow*, Faber and Faber.

8. THE MORAL

'We can now, perhaps, express his foreboding more precisely in psychological terms. Mankind, we can say, are committed to the process of expression, of differentiation. They cannot, for the sake of immediate power or comfort, reverse the process and try to be a herd or an army, without suffering quick spiritual and then material disaster through the suppression of desires which have become part of themselves and the very reasons why they wish to live.'

A. Clutton Brook: *The Necessity of Art*, S.C.M. Press.

Other titles from Notting Hill Editions*

Modern Buildings in London by Ian Nairn
Introduced by Travis Elborough

First published in 1964, *Modern Buildings in London* is a
celebration of the city's post-war architecture by the famously
untrained critic Ian Nairn. Written 'by a layman for laymen',
Nairn's take on 260 buildings that were instantly recognisable
as 'modern' includes descriptions of classic designs such as the
Barbican, the former BBC Television Centre, as well as schools,
ambulance stations, car parks and even care homes.

The last book in which Nairn approaches modern architecture
as the site of potential optimism, this alternative guidebook
maps out a lost London and shows Nairn writing at the pithy
peak of his powers.

'This book is something of a "ghost gazetteer", but it's not only
a period curiosity, and manages to speak more broadly to the
art of criticism itself as well as displaying Nairn's idiosyncratic
knack of recognising sheep and goats in London's post 1930s
re-fit.'
Times Literary Supplement

'This zesty guidebook, first published in 1964 for London
Transport, is the latest Ian Nairn classic to be given a hardback
makeover by Notting Hill Editions . . . For someone who
already owns one those vintage copies, the joy of this new
edition – following in the footsteps of *Nairn's Towns* and *Nairn's
Paris* – comes from writer and cultural commentator Travis
Elborough's informative and entertaining foreword . . .
This book makes both a fascinating gazetteer and nostalgia
trip.'
Twentieth-Century Society Magazine

Nairn's Paris by Ian Nairn
Introduced by Andrew Hussey

'About one third of this book is discovery, in the sense that I
came upon the sites by accident or by following a topographical
hunch. There must be many more, and all you need for the
search is the ability to turn off the main road, switch on your
antennae and respond. Good luck.' Ian Nairn

Out of print since 1968, *Nairn's Paris* is a unique guidebook
from the late, great architectural writer, Ian Nairn. Illustrated
with the author's black-and-white snaps of the city, Nairn gives
his readers an idiosyncratic and unpretentious portrait of the
'collective masterpiece' that is Paris. This guidebook shows his
eye for detail – whether it is architectural stonework on
an archway, shadows cast by a railing, or an empty chair in a
Paris park.

Nairn encourages the reader to find their own Paris beneath the
glossy surface – more than a guidebook, this is an inimitable
journey of discovery in finding the hidden delights of the city,
in the first hardback edition ever published.

'In *Nairn's Paris* the City of Light gets the flâneur it deserves:
passionate, bilious, eloquently melancholy . . . At his best
[Nairn] has no equal.'
David Collard

'A guidebook to the city of love like no other.'
The Connexion

Nairn's Towns by Ian Nairn
Introduced by Owen Hatherley

Nairn's Towns is a new edition of *Britain's Changing Towns*
by Ian Nairn (1967), introduced, edited and updated by Owen
Hatherley.

'These essays show him writing about cities and towns as
wholes rather than as collections of individual buildings.
In each of them, there are several things happening at once –
assessments of historic townscape, capsule reviews of
new buildings, attempts to find the specific character of each
place . . .'

Nairn's Towns contains sixteen short essays on places as varied
as Glasgow and Norwich, Llanidloes and Sheffield, by the finest
English architectural writer of the twentieth century.

'To call Ian Nairn a great architectural writer is too restrictive;
he was a great writer who happened to write about buildings
and places.'
Irish Times

'Once you discover [Nairn] you want to read everything he's
written.'
Daily Telegraph

'Nairn invented a way of looking, a way of writing.'
Jonathan Meades

'Should be kept in the glove-box of every car.'
Standpoint

Junkspace with *Running Room*
by Rem Koolhaas and Hal Foster

Junkspace with *Running Room* brings together two
groundbreaking essays in one edition. In *Junkspace* (2001),
architect Rem Koolhaas itemised in delirious detail how our
cities are being overwhelmed. His celebrated jeremiad is here
updated and twinned with *Running Room*, a fresh response
from architectural critic Hal Foster.

'The manifesto is a modernist mode, one that looks to
the future . . . *Junkspace* makes no such claim: "Architecture
disappeared in the twentieth century," states Koolhaas matter-
of-factly. *Junkspace* does a harder thing: it "foretells" the
present, which is to say that it calls on us to recognise what is
already everywhere around us.'
Hal Foster

'*Junkspace* is the new flamboyant, flexible, forgettable face
of architecture, rendered by Rem Koolhaas in a visceral and
rampantly analytical essay.'
Office for Metropolitan Architecture

'*Junkspace* is the most important piece of writing on
architecture of the 21st Century.'
Icon

*All titles are available in the UK, and some titles are
available in the rest of the world. For more information please
visit www.nottinghilleditions.com.

A selection of our titles is distributed in the US and
Canada by New York Review Books. For more information on
available titles please visit www.nyrb.com